HOLY WEEK and EASTER CEREMONIES and DRAMAS from MEDIEVAL SWEDEN

edited by
Audrey Ekdahl Davidson

Early Drama, Art, and Music
Monograph Series, 13

Medieval Institute Publications
WESTERN MICHIGAN UNIVERSITY
Kalamazoo, Michigan
1990

Printed in the United States of America

ISBN 0-918720-36-2 casebound
ISBN 0-918720-37-0 paperback

Contents

Illustrations

1. Easter Sepulcher in north wall of chancel. Kiaby, Skåne.

2. The Visit of the Holy Women to the Sepulcher. Linköping Cathedral.

3. Sepulcher with corpus formerly used in Good Friday and Easter ceremonies. Mariager, Denmark.

4. Matins and *Visitatio Sepulchri* (No. 1) in fragment of Linköping Ordinal (Riksarkivet, Värmland 1589, No. 12).

5. Matins (incomplete) and *Visitatio Sepulchri* (No. 2) in fragment of Linköping Antiphonal (Riksarkivet, Småland 1574, No. 3:2).

6. *Visitatio Sepulchri* (No. 3) from a Gradual possibly from the Stockholm area (Riksarkivet, Dalarna 1575, No. 14).

7-8. Matins, *Elevatio Crucis*, and *Visitatio Sepulchri* (No. 4) from a Vadstena Ordinal (Riksarkivet, Skoklostersammlingen, No. 2 [E 8899], pp. hi-hii).

9-10. *Visitatio Sepulchri* (No. 5) from a Linköping Breviary (Riksarkivet, Älfsborg/Lödöse 1575-1581).

11-12. Matins, *Elevatio Crucis*, and *Visitatio Sepulchri* (No. 6) from a Linköping Ordinal (1493) (Uppsala Universitets Biblioteket, MS. C. 428, fol. 37).

13-17. *Depositio Crucis* and *Elevatio Crucis* (No. 7) from a Vadstena Processional (Uppsala Universitets Biblioteket, MS. C. 506, fols. b ii-b iv [9ᵛ-11ᵛ]).

18. *Inuentor rutili* (incomplete) from Uppsala Universitets Biblioteket, MS. C. 506, fol. b viii (15ᵛ).

Acknowledgements

This book began as a search for concert material to be used with the group that I direct, the Society for Old Music. This organization, devoted to the performance of early (primarily pre-Bach) music, had previously performed the Easter drama *Visitatio sepulchri* in two versions, one from the *Fleury Playbook* and the other from a Hungarian manuscript. The *Visitatio sepulchri* has been said to embody the germ of Western liturgical music-drama, the *Quem queritis* dialogue between the Holy Women and angels at the empty tomb of Christ. Discovering the existence of such Easter dramas and related ceremonies in Sweden was appealing to me for personal reasons, since my grandparents were born in Scandinavia and had emigrated to the United States in the nineteenth century.

A previous research project focused on the Scandinavian St. John Passion from the sixteenth and seventeenth centuries had taken me to Sweden in 1977. That project, which also started as research for a concert, culminated in the volume entitled *The Quasi-Dramatic St. John Passions from Scandinavia and Their Medieval Background* (1981). At that time it became obvious to me that there was much medieval musical material available for performance and research from Swedish sources.

In taking up another Scandinavian project, I chose to transcribe the manuscripts and fragments containing Holy Week and Easter ceremonies and dramas which had performance possibilities. I found, however, that the fragments in particular, whether performable or not, were most at risk from deterioration, and therefore I decided to transcribe the entire known corpus of Swedish Holy Week and Easter dramas and quasi-dramatic ceremonies; however, only Nos. 5 and 7 were used in the 1988 performance for the local community and for the International Congress on Medieval Studies.

In addition to the transcriptions of texts and music, I have provided critical commentary for each. English translations of biblical passages were adapted from the Douay-Rheims translation of the Vulgate Bible, and most of the other translations were cheerfully provided by

E. Rozanne Elder, Director of the Cistercian Institute at Western Michigan University.

Many other people have aided me in my research. I am especially grateful to Ritva Jacobsson, Gunilla Iversen, and Gunilla Björkvall of the Corpus Troporum at the University of Stockholm for their assistance and kindnesses while I was engaged in research in Stockholm and at other times. Viveca Servatius, William Eifrig, Clyde Brockett, Jr., Michael Norton, and Fletcher Collins, Jr., read the manuscript in its entirety and made valuable suggestions. Otto Gründler of the Medieval Institute and Thomas Seiler of Medieval Institute Publications encouraged my work. Ann-Marie Nilsson of the Royal Academy of Music in Stockholm provided me with an opportunity for discussing the manuscripts and fragments with librarians and scholars directly interested in the material. Librarians and archivists at Riksarkivet in Stockholm, particularly Dr. Helmut Backhaus and Rut Hansen; at the University Library at Uppsala, especially Monica Hedlund and Inga Johansson; and at Lund University Library have all helped me with portions of the research. The musicians of the Society for Old Music helped me to understand the music-dramas and ceremonies better. Juleen Eichinger and Candace Woodruff were instrumental in producing the physical book.

But it is to my husband, Clifford Davidson, that I owe the greatest debt, for without his assistance I would not have been able to travel to libraries and archives in order to assemble this book. I would also like to acknowledge the debt I owe my family in instilling a love of and respect for things Scandinavian, and thus I dedicate this volume to my three sisters, Lorraine, Ione, and Lucille, and to the memory of my parents, Harry and Lydia Nelson Ekdahl.

I am grateful also to the Division of Research and Sponsored Programs at Western Michigan University for summer fellowships and grants in support of my research; a sabbatical leave enabled me to prepare my manuscript; and a final travel grant in the summer of 1989 enabled me to recheck my sources, especially No. 2 in which further deterioration of the binding now allowed me to see some notes and clef signs that had not been visible previously.

Permission to use the texts, musical transcriptions, and facsimiles has been kindly granted by Riksarkivet in Stockholm and by the Uppsala University Library. For assistance with the photographs of the

Easter sepulchers at Kiaby and Mariager I would like to thank Bengt Hernsell and Flemming and Birgit Poulsen. Permissions to use the illustrations of these Easter sepulchers in this book have been granted by the Rev. Veste Brynnestam of Kiaby and by the sacristan, Mr. Vagn Andreasen, and Church Council of Mariager. The photograph of the sculpture at Linköping Cathedral is used by permission of Antikvarisk-Topografiska Arkivet, Stockholm.

Abbreviations

The following abbreviations are used in the notes, especially in the identification of sources of the expansions of texts for which only incipits are given in the manuscripts:

AM: *Antiphonale monasticum pro diurnis horis* (Paris, Tournai, Rome: Desclée, 1934).

AS: *Antiphonale Sarisburiense*, ed. Walter Howard Frere (1901-24; rpt. Farnborough, Hants.: Gregg Press, 1966), 6 vols.

BrL: *Breviarium Lincopense*, ed. Knut Peters (Lund: Laurentius Petri Sällskapet, 1950-58), 4 vols.

BSV: *Biblia Sacra iuxta Vulgatam Versionem*, 3rd ed., ed. Robert Weber (Stuttgart: Deutsche Bibelgesellschaft, 1983).

CAO: *Corpus Antiphonalium Officii*, ed. Renato-Joanne Hesbert, Rerum Ecclesiasticarum Documenta, Ser. Mai. 10 (Rome: Herder, 1963-79), 6 vols.

GR: *Graduale sacrosancte Romanae ecclesiae* (Paris, Tournai, Rome: Desclée, 1974).

LC: *Liber Cantus* (Uppsala, 1620).

Lipphardt: Walther Lipphardt, *Lateinische Osterfeiern und Osterspiel* (Berlin: Walter de Gruyter, 1975-81), 6 vols.

LU: *The Liber Usualis* (Tournai and New York: Desclée, 1961).

Schmid: Toni Schmid, "Das Osterspiel in Schweden," *Kyrkohistorisk Årsskrift*, 52 (1952), 1-14.

WA: *Antiphonaire monastique; XIIIe siècle: Codex F. 160 de la bibliothèque de la cathédrale de Worcester*, Paléographie musicale, 12 (Tournai, 1922).

Translations from biblical texts are taken from the Douay-Rheims version: *The Holy Bible translated from the Latin Vulgate* (Baltimore: John Murphy, 1914).

Introduction

Medieval Sweden, in the remote northernmost reaches of Western Christendom, possessed quasi-dramatic ceremonies and dramas for Good Friday and Easter quite closely connected to the forms present in Germany, England, and other countries further south. Nevertheless, the Swedish ceremonies are sufficiently unique to merit scholarly attention in themselves. While the number of examples of such ceremonies and plays is not large, they do, however, comprise a rather neat geographical unit that can be studied. None of the examples from Sweden is particularly early, the earliest being of the thirteenth century.[1] Thus we are dealing with ceremonies and dramas that are entirely from the latter part of the Middle Ages—in other words, none at all as early as those contained in the *Regularis Concordia*, the English texts that are among the oldest to be preserved.[2] But since Sweden had only been fully Christianized in the eleventh and twelfth centuries, the earliest manuscript fragments containing the text of the Easter liturgical drama (Nos. 1-3) may be seen to

---

[1]For the date of the manuscripts and fragments containing the dramas and ceremonies, I have accepted the dating established by Toni Schmid, "Das Osterspiel in Schweden," *Kyrkohistorisk Årsskrift*, 52 (1952), 1-14; see also Walther Lipphardt, *Lateinische Osterfeiern und Osterspiele* (Berlin: Walter De Gruyter, 1975-81), II, 651-60, and VI, 431-32, 450-51.

[2]Pamela Sheingorn, *The Easter Sepulchre in England*, Early Drama, Art, and Music, Reference Ser., 5 (Kalamazoo: Medieval Institute Publications, 1987), pp. 18-21, figs. 1-4.

be genuine treasures of the Swedish people.

There are four kinds of quasi-dramatic and dramatic ceremonies extant in manuscripts from Sweden. The first is the quasi-dramatic chanting of the Passion story from St. John's Gospel which developed especially during the Reformation but which was based on medieval practice. From earlier in the Middle Ages, the Gospel for Good Friday was chanted not by a single deacon but by several clergy taking the various roles (e.g., the priest as Christ, the deacon as the Evangelist, and the sub-deacon as the crowd and the remaining characters). In the *Missale Lundense* printed in 1514 there are also directions in the rubrics for some dramatic action during the reading, as when, at the words "They parted my vestments among them" (*Partiti sunt vestimenta mea*), two acolytes furtively strip the altar of the altar cloths and appear to flee with them (*in modum furantis rapte abscondantur*). The Scandinavian Passion and its music have been discussed elsewhere,[3] however, and hence will not be given treatment in the present work.

Following the Mass of the Presanctified and the Adoration of the Cross on Good Friday there was another quasi-dramatic ceremony, the *Depositio crucis* in which the burial of Christ is represented. It was normal in Western rites to use a consecrated Host along with a figure of Christ, often

---

[3]Audrey Ekdahl Davidson, *The Quasi-Dramatic St. John Passions from Scandinavia and Their Medieval Background*, Early Drama, Art, and Music, Monograph Ser., 3 (Kalamazoo: Medieval Institute Publications, 1981); for the *Missale Lundense*, see pp. 27-28. Lund, in Skåne, was in the sixteenth century a province in Denmark since it had not yet been annexed to Sweden.

attached to a cross, for the burial.[4] Then on Easter morning there was also a ceremony which represented the Resurrection; this was the *Elevatio crucis*, when it was customary to remove the cross and Host from the place of burial. The high point of Easter morning, however, must have been the dramatic ceremony called the *Visitatio sepulchri* in which there is a representation of the visit of the Marys to the place of burial, now to be regarded as empty. The six examples from medieval Swedish service books suggest the popularity of this drama in Sweden, though only in one case is there an example of anything more than the briefest type of this play. Nowhere is there anything in the Swedish examples comparable to the complexity of the liturgical play on this subject from the *Fleury Playbook*, but unlike the Fleury *Visitatio* the Swedish plays are (with one exception) firmly attached to the service of Matins for Easter morning.

The *Depositio, Elevatio,* and *Visitatio sepulchri* all utilize a single *locus*, the sepulcher or tomb which represents the grave of Christ. The sepulcher may be a dual-purpose recess in the north wall of the chancel, a temporary chest-type structure, a combination donor tomb and sepulcher,[5] or a holy

---

[4]Only a cross is mentioned in the *Regularis Concordia* (Sheingorn, pp. 19-20), but the inclusion of a Host was common in later practice. For speculation regarding the origins of this practice, see O. B. Hardison, Jr., *Christian Rite and Christian Drama in the Middle Ages* (Baltimore: Johns Hopkins Press, 1965), p. 138; he suggests that there may have been two ceremonies that merged, or that there might have been an objection to the burial of the Host alone, since "the consecrated Host, being the living Christ, cannot be 'buried'."

[5]For the types of Easter sepulchers, see Sheingorn, pp. 35-36, 39-42; and on Swedish aumbries and Easter sepulchers, see Hans Hildebrand, *Sveriges Medeltid* (Stockholm, 1879-1903), III, 314-27, 647-49. For predominantly Danish examples, see Ulla Haastrup, "Medieval Props in the Liturgical Drama," *Hafnia,*

grave like one reported to be in the west part of Uppsala Cathedral in 1448.[6] An example of the recess is the aumbry-Easter Sepulcher at Kiaby in Skane (fig. 1), where the opening, which is not large, is enhanced by a wall painting of the Ascension that covers the side of the chancel. A free-standing tomb, however, is suggested in a sculpture showing the Marys at the tomb in Linköping Cathedral (fig. 2), while a post-Reformation description of practice in Uppland churches suggests a temporary structure.[7] Such a sepulcher from Vester-Löfsta is now in the Nordiska Museet in Stockholm.[8]

In Karl Young's generalized description of the *Depositio* ceremony he notes that it follows the scriptural account of the burial of Christ in the detail concerning the wrapping of the body in a linen cloth, according to the first three Gospels, and in linen cloths and spices, according to the Gospel of John. Although Jewish burial customs included both a shroud (*sudarium*) and linen cloths (*linteamina*), the medieval ceremony often uses a single cloth.[9] An excellent description of the ceremony is given in an account describing the rites at Durham in England. Here two elderly monks carry the crucifix along with a picture of Christ, on a gold-embroidered vel-

---

No. 11 (1987), pp. 138-46.

[6]Hildebrand, p. 648.

[7]Hildebrand, p. 647, as quoted in translation in Frederick J. Marker and Lise-Lone Marker, *The Scandinavian Theatre: A Short History* (Totowa, N.J.: Rowman and Littlefield, 1975), p. 2.

[8]Haastrup, pp. 145-46; Graham D. Caie, "Scandinavia," in *A Companion to the Medieval Theatre*, ed. Ronald W. Vince (New York: Greenwood Press, 1989), p. 310.

[9]Karl Young, *The Drama of the Medieval Church* (Oxford: Clarendon Press, 1933), I, 134-35.

vet cushion, "to the SEPULCHRE with great reverence, which Sepulchre was sett upp in the morninge, on the north side of the Quire, nigh to the High Altar, before the service time; and there lay it within the said Sepulchre, with great devotion, with another picture of our Saviour Christ, in whose breast they did enclose, with great reverence, the most holy and blessed Sacrament of the Altar, senceinge it and prayinge unto it upon theire knees, a great space, settinge two tapers lighted before it, which tapers did burne unto Easter day in the morninge, that it was taken forth."[10] Nothing so elaborate is described in the rubrics of the *Depositio* that appears in a single Swedish manuscript (No. 7). The rubrics tell little more than when the ceremony takes place: *In die parasceues finitis uesperis sororum quando crux portatur ad sepulchrum*, that is, at the end of the Sisters' Vespers (on Good Friday) when the cross is carried to the sepulcher. The participants are informed when to return from the sepulcher—*In reditu de sepulcro*—but no specifics regarding the location or the nature of the activities at the sepulcher are given. Within the *Depositio* service there is also a marginal addition of a rubric referring to the hymn *Inuentor rutili*. Though the rubrics of the *Depositio* do not specify exactly the actions that accompany the music, from analogy with other ceremonies—e.g., those found in English sources like the *Regularis Concordia* or the Durham ceremonial—we know that there must be a symbolic burial of the cross and also possibly a Host.

---

[10]*A Description or Breife Declaration of All the Ancient Monuments, Rites, and Customes Belonginge or Beinge within the Monastical Church of Durham before the Suppression*, Surtees Soc. (London, 1844 [for 1842]), p. 10.

The Corpus of the dead Redeemer might be life-size.[11]

The chants for the *Depositio* include the responsory *Ecce quomodo moritur,* the verse *In pace factus est,* the antiphon *Caro mea requiescet in spe,* the antiphon *In pace factus est,* the responsory *Sepulto Domino signatum est monumentum,* and another melodic setting of the verse *In pace factus est.* The text of the first responsory treats the theme of the "just man," in an allusion to Christ "who is offered up in the face of wickedness," while the verses and antiphons continue with the reassurances that "His abode is established in peace" and that "My flesh shall rest in hope." *Sepulto Domino* describes the sealing of the tomb and the setting of the soldiers before it to guard it in an apparent triumph for the *adversarius,* as Hardison notes.[12]

Though the form of the *Depositio* varies with geographical location, the Swedish selection of chants is not unusual, nor are the melodic forms of the chants particularly unique. For example, the general contour of *Sepulto Domino* and *Caro mea requiescet* as well as the antiphon version of *In pace factus est* will be found to match the chants found in the Sarum Processional printed by Pynson in 1502.[13] The Swedish *Depositio* does not include the antiphon *In pace in idipsum* which is found in several sources nor the antiphon

---

[11]Hildebrand, p. 648 and fig. 536; Haastrup, pp. 140-47.
[12]Hardison, p. 138.
[13]*Processionale ad Usum Sarum* (facs. rpt. Clarabricken: Boethius Press, 1980), sigs. I1ᵛ-I2ʳ.

Habitabit in tabernaculo, which is less frequently found.[14]

As noted above, the Swedish Depositio ceremony (No. 7) has a marginal reference to the hymn *Inuentor rutili*, a hymn which is to be found later in the manuscript (at fol. b viii).[15] The rubric, coming between the words *custodirent* and *illud*[16] and interrupting the flow of the responsory *Sepulto Domino*, directs that this hymn be used "after the blessing of the new fire." Although in some churches, for example the church at Evesham in England, the lighting of the new fire could be done on each of the three days—Maundy Thursday, Good Friday, and Holy Saturday[17]—the rubric in the Swedish manuscript clearly indicates that it was kindled on Holy Saturday. Thus, this rubric must have been omitted from its rightful place in the ceremony for Holy Saturday and instead was squeezed into the Good Friday service by a scribe trying to find a location for the rubric. The hymn itself is found later in the manuscript and is thus not directly relevant to the

---

[14]*In pace in idipsum* and *Habitabit in tabernaculo* are part of the *Depositio* text in the *Regularis Concordia* (Young, I, 133); *In pace in idipsum* is found in other sources—e.g., a thirteenth-century Gradual from Rouen (Young, I, 135). For possible musical settings for these chants, see *Liber Usualis*, p. 752. In the *Breviarium Lincopense*, ed. Knut Peters (Lund: Laurentius Petri Sällskapet, 1950-58), the antiphons *In pace in idipsum* and *Habitabit in tabernaculo* appear in the liturgy for Matins on Holy Saturday (II, Pt. 2, 371).

[15]For the rubric see the Appendix to No. 7, below. At fol. b viii, there is another rubric, which indicates that the hymn is to be used on Holy Saturday after the blessing of the new fire. As for the hymn itself, after two stanzas it breaks off at the bottom of b viii (fol. 15^v); an *Alleluia* is at the top of the next folio. There appears to be a lacuna, for the middle leaf of a quire of five double leaves has apparently fallen out; I am indebted to Monica Hedlund and Inga Johansson of the Uppsala Universitetsbibliotek for this information.

[16]Cf. *Liber Usualis*, p. 773, which gives *illum* for the MS. *illud*.

[17]See John Walton Tyrer, *Historical Survey of Holy Week: Its Services and Ceremonial* (London: Oxford Univ. Press, 1932), p. 149.

study of the *Depositio*.

Elevatio ceremonies are found in three of the Swedish manuscripts: Nos. 4, 6, and 7. In each of these, the *Elevatio* precedes the service of Matins for Easter Sunday. Again, actual directions for performing the ceremonies are sparse, though English and European *Elevatio* ceremonies commonly specify the bringing forth of the cross (and in some cases, the Host as well) from the sepulcher in re-enactment of the resurrection of Christ. The description from Durham again is one of the most complete accounts:

> two of the oldest Monkes of the Quire came to the Sepulchre . . . , all covered with red velvett and embrodered with gold, and then did sence it, either Monke with a pair of silver sencers sittinge on theire knees before the Sepulchre. Then they both rising came to the Sepulchre, out of the which, with great devotion and reverence, they tooke a marvelous beautifull IMAGE OF OUR SAVIOUR, representing the resurrection, with a crosse in his hand, in the breast wherof was enclosed in bright christall the holy Sacrament of the Altar, throughe the which christall the Blessed Host was conspicuous to the behoulders. Then, after the elevation of the said picture, carryed by the said two Monkes uppon a faire velvett cushion, all embrodered, singinge the anthem of *Christus resurgens*, they brought it to the High Altar, settinge that on the midst therof, whereon it stood, the two Monkes kneelinge on theire knees before the Altar, and senceing it all the time that the rest of the whole quire was in singing the foresaid anthem of *Christus resurgens*. The which anthem beinge ended, the two Monkes tooke up the cushions and the picture from the Altar, supportinge it be-

twixt them, proceeding, in procession, from the High Altar to the south Quire dore, where there was four antient Gentlemen, belonginge to the Prior, appointed to attend theire cominge, holdinge upp a most rich CANNOPYE of purple velvett, tached round about with redd silke and gold fringe; and at everye corner did stand one of theise ancient Gentlemen, to beare it over the said image, with the Holy Sacrament, carried by two Monkes round about the church, the whole quire waitinge uppon it with goodly torches and great store of other lights, all singinge, rejoyceinge, and praising God most devoutly, till they came to the High Altar againe, wheron they did place the said image there to remaine untill the Ascension day.[18]

The Swedish *Elevatio* ceremonies, which lack the *Christus resurgens* found at Durham, begin with *Surrexit Dominus* and proceed next to the three stanzas from the hymn *Ad coenam agni providi*[19] (*Cum surgit Christus, Quesumus auctor,* and *Gloria tibi*). *Surrexit Dominus* signals the actual elevation of the cross or image, while the *Cum surgit* stanza from *Ad coenam agni providi* refers to Christ's resurrection and to his having returned "as a victor from hell"—a reference to the theme of the Harrowing of Hell which will be treated more fully in the last antiphon, *Cum rex glorie. Quesumus auctor* is a plea to the "Creator of all," a request that Christ's

---

[18]*A Description or Breife Declaration,* pp. 10-11.

[19]For the text of *Ad coenam agni providi,* see *Breviarium Lincopense,* II, Pt. 2, 387, and *Analecta Hymnica,* II, 46, as quoted by Young, I, 562. The melody for the hymn which is closest to the Swedish incipits will be found in Bruno Stäblein, *Hymnen: Die mittelalterlichen Hymnenmelodien des Abendlandes,* Monumenta monodica medii aevi, 1 (Kassel and Basel: Bärenreiter, 1956), I, 189. For Stäblein's source, see *Paléographie musicale,* XII. *Ad coenam* is for use in the octave of Easter as well as on Ascension at Vespers.

people might be defended from the onslaught of death; *Gloria tibi* expresses praise to the risen Lord.

The Harrowing of Hell theme, ultimately derived from the apocryphal Gospel of Nicodemus and only hinted at in the *Cum surgit* stanza, receives elaboration, as noted above, in *Cum rex glorie*. In the Gospel of Nicodemus, in this instance paraphrasing Psalm 23(24).7, Christ's voice, "the voice of a great thunder," proclaims the following motif, with slight variations, three times: "Lift up, ye princes, your gates, and be ye lift up, ye everlasting doors, and the King of glory shall come in." Following the third statement of this command, Hell itself quakes, all the locks of the gates are broken, and the gates of Hell are opened. Then Christ enters Hell "in the glory of the light of the height, in meekness, great and yet humble," and Satan is bound in fetters, while the patriarchs are set free and brought to paradise.[20] The antiphon *Cum rex glorie* in the *Elevatio* describes Christ's entrance into hell and his reception by those—including Adam, Eve, David, and the other patriarchs and prophets—whom he has come to rescue. Those who have been sitting in darkness cry out, "You have come, desired of nations, for whom we in chains have waited in darkness to lead us this night from prison." They designate him "the hope of the desolate" and "the great consolation of those in torment." The inclusion of the Harrowing of Hell episode in the *Elevatio* involves liturgical reflection on an event which has occurred, since Christ's descent into

---

[20]*The Apocryphal New Testament*, trans. M. R. James (Oxford: Clarendon Press, 1924), pp. 132-40 (Latin B text).

the underworld was thought to have taken place between his death and his resurrection. However, in this position in the *Elevatio* it identifies the bringing of light and life to the holy dead who had been languishing in hell as analogous to the bringing of light and life to all mankind by means of the Resurrection on Easter.[21]

The Swedish post-Reformation account to which reference has been made above describes, though not without a certain lack of precision, the ceremonies of Good Friday and Easter in an Uppland church:

> They used to come to church early on Easter morning so that the women could anoint Jesus, whose image of stone or wood was laid out in a crypt, which was formed like a sepulchre and placed by the altar, and upon which a guardian angel was seated. This I have seen in two churches in Uppland such as Vada and Skarplöfstad [Vester-Löfsta]. They oiled the image with fragrant balsam, traces of which are still to be found on the above-mentioned crypt. They also crawled on their knees around these sepulchres to do penance for their sins.[22]

---

[21]The Harrowing was enacted dramatically along with the *Elevatio* at Barking in England during the tenure of Abbess Katherine of Sutton (1363-76). Young describes the re-enactment: "Behind the closed doors of [the chapel of Mary Magdalene] are imprisoned all the members of the convent, representing the souls of the patriarchs confined in Hell and awaiting the coming of Christ. After the priest outside has uttered *Tollite portas* three times, the door of the chapel is flung open, and all the imprisoned spirits, carrying palms of victory, are allowed to depart in procession toward the sepulchre during the singing of several antiphons, the last of which is *Cum rex glorie*" (I, 167).

[22]Hildebrand, *Sveriges Medeltid*, III, 647, as quoted in translation by Marker and Marker, p. 2.

The apparent anointing of the image on Good Friday here seems to be conflated with the coming of the Holy Women to the sepulcher on Easter morning and their meeting with the angel. The latter episode is, of course, the one dramatized in the *Visitatio sepulchri*, which is intended to make visible the events of the first Easter for the congregation.

Of the six examples of the *Visitatio sepulchri* extant in Swedish manuscripts (Nos. 1-6), three (Nos. 1, 4, and 6) have either complete or virtually complete Matins services for Easter preceding the drama; No. 2 utilizes *Dum transisset, Et valde,* and *Te Deum,* while No. 5 has only *Maria Magdalena et alia Maria* as the opening item of the drama as well as the *Te Deum* at the end. There are no vestiges of Matins connected with No. 3. With five out of six Swedish *Visitatio sepulchri* manuscripts being connected with at least some aspects of Matins, the persistence of the placing of the drama following Matins seems to indicate a normal practice.

In Nos. 1, 4, and 6, each of the items of the Matins service is directly appropriate to the Easter theme. The service usually begins with texts that are appropriate at any time of the year—*Domine labia mea, Deus in adjutorium meum,* and the Invitatory, Psalm 94 (*Venite, exultemus Domino*)—and also includes the appointed psalms for the Sunday office. Psalm 1 (*Beatus vir*) introduces "the just man," terminology which recalls the typological reference to Christ in *Ecce quomodo moritur,* while Psalm 2 (*Quare fremuerunt*) makes reference to the "kings of the earth" who "stood up . . . against the Lord, and against his Christ"—a prediction of the Passion of Christ, which culminated in his crucifixion. Psalm 3 (*Domini quid multiplicati*) with its antiphon, *Ego dormivi*, prophesies the Resurrection: "I have slept and have taken my rest: and I have risen up. . . ." Material even more specifically associated with the Easter events is introduced with the use of the responsory *Quem queris mulier* ("Whom seek ye, woman") in Nos. 1, 4, and 6.

But it is through the lessons from the Gospel of Mark and from Gregory's commentary on it (not quoted but only indicated in Nos. 1, 4, and 6) that the Easter events are most explicitly delineated and explained. In verses 1-8 of the sixteenth chapter of the Gospel according to Mark, the entire story is recounted: how the women (Mary Magdalene, Mary the mother of James, and Salome)[23] brought spices to the sepulcher in order to anoint Jesus, and how at the tomb they found an angel[24] who told them that Christ was not there but had risen. Their reaction in *Mark* was to flee in fear—a detail

---

[23]While the Gospel according to Mark (16.1) lists Mary Magdalene, Mary the mother of James, and Salome, in the accounts given in the other three Gospels the names and number of women vary as follows: in *Matthew* 28.1, the women are Mary Magdalene and the other Mary (*et altera Maria*); in *Luke* 24.10, the women are identified as Mary Magdalene, Joanna, and Mary, the mother of James; in *John* 20.1, only Mary Magdalene is mentioned. The Swedish versions of the drama also vary: in No. 3, the number of women is not specified; in No. 5, two Marys are mentioned—Mary Magdalene and the other Mary (*alia Maria*). In the other manuscripts (Nos. 1, 2, 4, and 6), three clergy as women are specified. The names of the women are, however, only listed in the antiphon *Dum transisset*, which follows *Mark*.

[24]In *Mark* 16.1, the women encounter a young man who is wearing a white garment and who can only be an angel, while in *Matthew* 28.5 the figure is clearly labeled an angel (*angelus*). *Luke* 24.4 describes two men in shining garments who tell the women that Christ is risen. In the Gospel according to John, chap. 20, there is no mention of angels. In the Swedish versions of the *Visitatio* which contain rubrics, two angels are usually specified.

which is omitted in the Swedish examples of the *Visitatio sepulchri.*

Gregory the Great's homily "relates the visit to the tomb to the lives of the faithful," as Hardison notes. Further, "The holy women are symbols of devotion, and all Christians should imitate them: '. . . this that they did, teaches what we, the members of the Church, should do . . . if laden with the fragrance of virtue and the reputation of good works, we seek the Lord, we may truly be said to come to the sepulcher with sweet spices. Moreover, the women, who came with sweet spices, saw angels; and those souls come to the vision of the heavenly citizens, who, fragrant in virtue, tend to the Lord by their holy desires'."[25]

Further, Hardison notes that this commentary on the passage in *Mark* which treats the women's bringing spices in order to anoint Christ is followed by a series of responsories and verses in harmony with the drama at the sepulcher: "The angel of the Lord came down from heaven, and as he came closer, he rolled away the stone and sat upon it. And he said to the women, 'Fear not. I know that you seek the crucified one. He is risen. Come and see the place where the Lord was laid'." The next responsory is also very closely related to the first one. *Dum transisset* retells the story of the three women—Mary Magdalene, Mary the mother of James, and Salome—coming to the sepulcher, as does the verse which follows (*Et valde mane*).

---

[25]Hardison, p. 171, citing Gregory's homily from Prosper Guéranger, *Liturgical Year*, VII, 118-21. The selections from this homily and their placement in the texts edited below follow *Breviarium Lincopense*, II, Pt. 2, 375.

The reiteration of *Dum transisset* leads directly to the famous *Quis reuoluet-Quem queritis* dialogue, which is the kernel of the drama as well as the most significant musical material. It has been likened to "a precious jewel in the Easter liturgy,"[26] and it has immense import in the history of drama.

The *Visitatio* story is well known. The women, who at first do not know that the stone has already been rolled away, ask, *Quis reuoluet nobis ab hostio lapidem* ("Who will roll the stone away from the door for us?"). Instead of answering, the angels seated within the tomb pose another question: *Quem queritis in sepulchrum* ("Whom do you seek in the tomb?"). The women answer, *Jesum Nazarenum crucifixum* ("Jesus of Nazareth, crucified"), to which the angels reply, *Non est hic; sed surrexit sicut praedixerat* ("He is not here; he is risen as he said he would").[27] At this point, the

---

[26]Gunilla Iversen, "Aspects of the Transmission of the *Quem Quaeritis*," *Text*, 3 (1987), 155-82, esp. 155. In her article, Iversen deals with the vexed question of whether the *Quem queritis* was "a trope to the introit antiphon *Resurrexi* at Easter Mass," or "part of a procession preceding the Mass," or "an autonomous verse of the Mass, unconnected with the introit," or "from the beginning a part of the *Visitatio sepulchri* ceremony at the end of Matins and thus followed by the *Te Deum*" (p. 157). Her conclusion is that we do not know, but that she would "not be surprised if in the end we come back to the thesis of Helmut de Boor and others that the QQ was originally an independent verse in the form of a dialogue, performed as an alternate song, an introduction to the whole Easter Mass." As a highly knowledgeable researcher, she finds it a challenge to study further the dialogue and "to identify the different liturgical, esthetic and literary demands to which the *Quem quaeritis* in its various forms was made the answer" (p. 179).

[27]David Bjork has argued that the exchange between the women—*Quem queritis in sepulchro, Christicole*; *Jhesum Nazarenum crucifixum, o celicole*; and *Non est hic, surrexit sicut predixerat. Ite nunciate quia surrexit de sepulchro*—is the essential element in the *Visitatio* ("On the Dissemination of *Quem quaeritis* and the *Visitatio sepulchri* and the Chronology of Their Early Sources," *Comparative*

angels' invitation *Venite et videte locum, ubi positus erat Dominus* ("Come and see the place where the Lord was laid") is found in all six Swedish examples of the *Visitatio sepulchri*. In Nos. 1, 2, 4, and 6, the antiphon *Cito euntes dicite discipulis et petro quia surrexit Dominus* ("Go quickly and tell the disciples and Peter that the Lord is risen") is then added. According to Young, this antiphon serves as a second dismissal in addition to *Venite et videte*.[28] While the music of No. 5 is of the less complex (Type I) variety, its text represents a uniquely more elaborate (technically known as Type II[29]) *Visitatio* including the race of Peter and John. It lacks *Cito euntes* but adds *Ad monumentum uenimus gementes* ("Mourning we came to the grave site"), *Currebant duo simul* ("The two ran together," a description of the race of the disciples),[30] and *Cernitis o socii ecce linteamina et sudarium et corpus non est inuentum* ("Behold, O companions, the winding sheet and the napkin, but the body is not found"); none of these is present in any other Swedish source. Nos. 1, 2, 3,

---

Drama, 14 [1980], 46). Since *Quis reuoluet* is included in many continental and all Swedish versions, I see no reason to exclude this item from among the essential elements of the drama germ as it appears in Sweden.

[28]Young, I, 252. The text of this antiphon in the expansions of incipits in the Swedish examples below differs slightly from the text quoted by Young since it is based on the variant in the *Breviarium Lincopense* (II, Pt. 1, 390)

[29]The other examples of the Swedish *Visitatio* are of the simple Type I variety. With regard to the form of the Type II *Visitatio*, see Michael Norton, "Of 'Stages' and 'Types' in *Visitatione Sepulchri*," *Comparative Drama*, 21 (1987), 34-61, 127-44.

[30]For the suggestion that *Currebant* was "borrowed . . . for use as most appropriate choral 'background music' to the Race" of Peter and John to the sepulcher, see William L. Smoldon, *The Music of the Medieval Church Dramas*, ed. Cynthia Bourgeault (London: Oxford Univ. Press, 1980), p. 160. See also the introduction to No. 5, below.

and 5 introduce *Surrexit Dominus* ("The Lord . . . is risen"). In place of the *Surrexit Dominus*, Nos. 4 and 6 use *Victime paschali*; the latter has, according to Hardison, the function of providing "dialogue for the scene, only mentioned in Scripture, in which the Marys tell the disciples of the Resurrection."[31] In all but one of the Swedish examples of the *Visitatio*, the *Te Deum* is sung, presumably along with a general censing.[32] In No. 3, however, there is no *Te Deum*, but a prayer appears: *Deus qui pro nobis filium tuum crucis patibulum subire uoluisti. et inimici a nobis expelleres potestatem concede nobis famulis tuis. ut in resurrectionis eius gaudiis semper uiuamus* ("O God, who for our sake was willing to submit your son to the gibbet of the cross, and who drove away from us the power of the enemy, grant that we, your servants, may always live in the joys of his resurrection.") At this point the fragment breaks off.

In the three *Visitatio* dramas with musical notation, the melodies used for the *Quis reuoluet* interrogation differ considerably. The melody for No. 2, readable only with great difficulty, begins with a rising fifth pattern.

No. 2 c   d d-a-b flat a a g-f g g-a a   a-c
    Quis re-uol-   uet no-bis la- pi- dem ab

     c-b   g-a   a a g-f g-a a
     hos-   ti-   o mo-nu- men-ti.

---

[31] Hardison, p. 237.
[32] See Young, I, 252.

No. 3 begins with a very static melody; at the words *Qvis reuoluat* (*sic*), the same note is reiterated except that there is an interpolation of an ornamental liquescent note that descends a tone on the word *Qvis*. *Nobis* descends on three adjacent notes, with *lapidem* beginning with the same notes as does *nobis* but descending one further note.

No. 3 f-f-e f f f f-e d f-e d c c-d-e d c c e-f < >
      Qvis re-uol-uat no-bis la-pi-dem ab os-ti-o mo-nu-men-ti.

Quis reuoluit in No. 5 has a rising fourth on the word *Quis*, giving it a contour which reverses that of the beginning of the *Quem queritis* settings in the Swedish manuscripts. *Reuoluit*, departing from the same tone on which *Quis* ends, from thence rises, falls, and rises again, with *nobis* and *ab hostio* repeating the same descending adjacent three-note pattern [bracketed]:

No. 5 g-c c d c [c-b a] [c-b a]-g g g-a a g f f
      Quis re- uol-uit no- bis ab hos- ti- o la- pi- dem quem

    g-a a a a-g-a-g g-e-f f-a-c b-c a-g-f g-a-a g g
    te- ge- re sanc- tum cer- ni- mus se- pul- chrum.[33]

Further analysis would reveal similar points of repetition—for example, the last syllable of *hostio* is set to the same

---

[33]For the text of this item, cf. *Corpus Antiphonalium Officii*, ed. Renato-Joanne Hesbert (Rome: Herder, 1963-79), No. 2697.

notes as the first syllable of *tegere*. *Sanctum* rocks back and forth on the same a-g interval that sets the first syllable of *hostio* and the first syllable of *tegere*.

Susan Rankin and others have noted the similarity of structure in the settings for *Quem queritis* and *Jhesum Nazarenum*. Each falls neatly into three parts, including "an intonation, median phrase and cadence." This means that there is a deliberate lack of differentiation between the music for women and angels; "diversity of heavenly interrogators and earthly seekers is not what the composer was after."[34] Thus differentiation of one type of character from another apparently was not considered important or necessary.

The setting for the angels' query in all three notated manuscripts begins with varying ways of utilizing the descending fourth, a most pervasive interval for this trope.[35] The shortest presentations of the familiar question are found in Nos. 2 and 3, which ask only *Quem queritis in sepulcro, o*

---

[34]Susan Rankin, "Musical and Ritual Aspects of *Quem queritis*," in *Liturgische Tropen*, ed. Gabriel Silagi, Münchener Beitrage zur Mediävistik und Renaissance-Forschung, 36 (München: Arbeo-Gesellschaft, 1985), pp. 190-91.

[35]It is beyond the scope of this study of the Swedish examples to attempt to show that the descending fourth pattern for *Quem queritis* within the *Visitatio* drama is the most characteristic setting in other European sources. Rankin notes that there are fifty-one versions datable before 1100 of the three sentences that have been said to make up the essence of the drama. One of these sentences is the *Quem queritis* trope, which in these early examples always has the same melody, beginning with the interval of the descending fourth ("Musical and Ritual Aspects of the *Quem queritis*," p. 190). And in the numerous examples of the *Quem queritis* dialogue which Smoldon presents (charts following p. 430), the descending fourth intervallic beginning for the melody seems to be predominant in France, Germany, and Spain. In some continental versions there is an interruption of a descending major second before the lower note is reached (g-f-d). This ornamental note is present only as a liquescent note in No. 3 of the Swedish examples.

christicole? No. 5 is more elaborate: *Quem queritis o tremule mulieres in hoc tumulo plorantes?* The three notated manuscripts are in essential agreement as to the setting of the initial two words, with a slight exception in the case of the word *Quem*, which is set to a g-d interval in No. 2, to two g's with a liquescent descending tone in No. 3, and to two g's in No. 5. The settings of the opening words of the question are compared below:

No. 2 g-d   d-f-e f-g g
       Quem que- ri- tis

No. 3 g   g-f d-f-e f-g g
       Quem que- ri- tis

No. 5 g-g   d-f-e f-g g
       Quem que- ri- tis

In each of the three manuscripts the music for the remainder of the statement bears some resemblance to the classic continental versions,[36] even though No. 5 has the elongated statement to set. The notes for *Ihesum Nazarenum* in No. 2 are readable only with difficulty, but they appear to be as follows:

---

[36]For one continental example—Paris, Bibliothèque Nationale, lat. 909, fols. 21ᵛ-22—see Bjork, p. 57.

No. 2 f-g g   f a c a   g f-e f-g f f
      Ihe-sum Na-za-re-num o ce- li- co-le.[37]

This passage, in its transposed state, follows the classic form found, for example in the Paris, Bibliothèque Nationale manuscript (MS. lat. 909, fols. 21ᵛ-22) cited by David Bjork.[38] The setting for *Ihesum Nazarenum* in No. 3 is entirely idiosyncratic, but the music for No. 5 again takes the classic form. The musical setting for the first two words, *Ihesum Nazarenum*, takes the opposite direction from the *Quem queritis* music, but the general structure echoes the *Quem queritis* music, as noted above.

No. 5 f-g g   f   a   c   a   c   g a-g f
      Ihe- sum Na- za- re- num cru- ci- fi- xum

Non est hic takes an entirely different direction from *Quem queritis*, with its ascending fifth pattern in the classical form and in two of the Swedish notated *Visitatio* manuscripts. (The setting for the first word of *Non est hic* is obscured in No. 3, and hence the notation cannot be ascertained.) However, Nos. 2 and 5 utilize the characteristic rising fifth as setting for these words. No. 2 delays the rising fifth until the word *hic*, while No. 5 arrives at the fifth in the

---

[37]See Alejandro Planchart, *The Repertory of Tropes at Winchester* (Princeton: Princeton Univ. Press, 1977), I, 238; Planchart locates the text form with *O celicole* as French and the version without *O* as found in Germany, Switzerland, and northern Italy.
[38]Bjork, p. 57.

first word, *Non.* No. 5 also has a four-note melisma on *hic.* It is to be observed that No. 3 is unconventional in many ways, perhaps owing to a loss of tradition or to a careless scribe.

For the most part, the music of the Swedish manuscripts and fragments is syllabic or neumatic, with no long melismatic passages. Both drama and music (when present) are very tight, economical, and lacking in extraneous material. The *Visitatio* contained in No. 5, however, is distinguished by the fact that it is the one with the most practical musical and dramatic potential.

We are not possessed of a great deal of information regarding performance practice of these Swedish Holy Week and Easter ceremonies and dramas; however, two terms are used within the plays to describe vocal color: *clara voce* (meaning clear, strong voice) and *submisse voce* (meaning low, soft voice). In Nos. 4 and 6 the angels (those seated within) sing to the holy women with a clear, strong voice, and later the women, holding up linen cloths and proceeding toward the people, sing in a clear, strong voice also. Nos. 4, 5, and 6 all begin the *Visitatio* with the clerics representing women singing the antiphon "Who will roll away from the door for us the stone which we saw covering the holy tomb?" in a low, soft voice. We also have some general directions to the Brigittine sisters regarding their manner while singing, for Birgitta's own adjurations to the sisters were that they should sing with *odmiuktinne* (humility). This information is attributed to Petrus Olavi, Birgitta's confessor and the per-son who helped to create the order of the Brigittine service.[39] We are left to speculate as to whether this meant that only their demeanor would be affected or whether the humility should take the form of a soft, sweet, "humble" vocal tone, perhaps the tone identified with the *submisse voce* of those representing the holy women in the plays.

As for the possible usage of instruments in the church service, we have the instance of the journey made in the latter part of the fifteenth century by Sten Sture, bishop of Linköping, who, accompanied by several Brigittine sisters, went to see the Danish Queen. It is related that pipes and sackbutts were played at Mass, undoubtedly with Bishop Sture's consent.[40] Surely there would have been no instruments in the Good Friday ceremonies, but would such instrumentation have been used for the festive Easter services—perhaps even for the *Elevatio* and *Visitatio*? In England, the Brigittine sisters and brothers of Syon Abbey in the mid-fifteenth century were permitted the use of sacring bells at Mass on Palm Sunday;[41] on Easter Day, "atte begynnyng of the resurreccion, al the bellys schal be ronge the space of oo miserere, whiche also schal stonde for the fyrst pele to matens, and than the ryngers schal hye them . . . to the worchyppyng of the crosse."[42] Perhaps identical practices were found in Sweden, since the order

---

[39]Tobias Norlind, *Bilder ur Svenska Musikens Historia fran älsta tid til medeltidens slut* (Stockholm: Musikhistoriska Museet, 1947), I, 174.
[40]Ibid., I, 174.
[41]George James Aungier, *The History and Antiquities of Syon Monastery, the Parish of Isleworth, and the Chapelry of Hounslow* (London: J. B. Nichols and Son, 1840), p. 345.
[42]Ibid., p. 353.

was, after all, Swedish in origin, and bells are explicitly indicated in several of the ceremonies included in this book though at a different point in the Easter festival.

By the end of the sixteenth century, the Reformation had taken hold in Sweden, and the *Depositio, Elevatio,* and *Visitatio Sepulchri* were no longer presented on Good Friday and Easter. The ceremonies and the drama had been proscribed in 1591. When the Polish king, Sigismund, visited Sweden in 1594, Roman Catholic priests performed the *Depositio* and *Elevatio* rites—rites which triggered popular antagonism.[43]

However, in the changed climate of the early seventeenth century, a reaction would set in. The *Liber Cantus*, printed at Uppsala in 1620, not only presents a wealth of fairly standard service music but also includes the Latin chants for Good Friday and Easter that had been utilized for the ceremonies and the drama, though there are no rubrics or other indications that the physical acts demanded by the medieval rites would have been preserved. Nevertheless, it is remarkable that so much music from the rites survived the Reformation. At the same time, the *Liber Cantus* preserves the Swedish forms of a number of the chants, which appear only as incipits in the medieval manuscripts and fragments.

Editorial Procedures. In editing the Swedish examples of the *Depositio, Elevatio,* and *Visitatio sepulchri,* I have found very useful the Guidelines for Transcription prepared by Records of Early English Drama. For each of the seven manu-

---

[43]Marker and Marker, p. 2.

scripts and fragments, a diplomatic text, without changes from the given manuscript except for expansion of abbreviations and incipits, is presented. For the four with notation, musical transcriptions are also given, with texts corrected and lightly modernized.

The principles of editing which I have adopted are indicated as follows, divided into those applied to the seven texts and those applied to the four musical transcriptions:

TEXTS

1. Expansions of abbreviations appear in italics. The abbreviation & is written as *et*.

2. The original spelling is retained. Letters and words crossed out are indicated, and scribal errors are not corrected. Capitalization is unchanged; size of capitals is not indicated.

3. No punctuation is added to the Latin texts.

4. It seemed neither practical nor necessary to follow the layout of the manuscripts exactly because of the inclusion in this book of facsimiles of the originals. Nevertheless, transcriptions of the texts include indication of page divisions by vertical lines.

5. Damaged or unreadable text is indicated by diamond brackets, thus: < >. Blank spaces are shown by italicized parentheses surrounding the blanks *( )*. Crossed out words or letters are rendered as in the manuscripts. Interlineations above the line are indicated by ⌈ ⌉.

6. When only incipits are given, additions and interpolations to the text from known sources are enclosed within square brackets surrounding the added material. The style of the orthography and punctuation in the bracketed material is retained, and the source in each case is listed in the notes.

7. Translations are provided following each text. The pointing of the translations follows modern practice.

MUSICAL TRANSCRIPTIONS

1. Since two of the manuscripts, Nos. 2 and 3, were either seriously damaged or so truncated as to be unperformable, the aim of these two transcriptions could not be to provide performance versions. Rather, these transcriptions are presented for purposes of study and comparison. The other two, Nos. 5 and 7, have genuine performance possibilities, and have been presented with that purpose in mind.

2. As noted above, the text underlay has been lightly modernized, with modern punctuation. All abbreviations have been expanded, and scribal errors silently corrected.

3. Damaged and obliterated text and notes are shown in diamond brackets: < >. Where a parallel source has been drawn upon, the notes from the source are placed within the brackets but without color ("white notes").

Finally, the plates contain facsimiles of all the ceremonies and plays that appear in Swedish manuscripts and
fragments so that scholars may see exactly how these have
been presented by the original scribes.

1

Visitatio Sepulchri
from a Linköping Ordinal

A Type I *Visitatio sepulchri* (containing only the scene of the women at the tomb) is included in a fragment consisting of two folios from an Ordinal from the Linköping diocese and dating from the thirteenth century. It is, as Toni Schmid notes,[1] the earliest fragment of liturgical drama in Sweden and owes its preservation in part to the fact that it is attached as covers to a volume of provincial records. The document is located in Riksarkivet, Stockholm, and filed as Värmland, 1589, No. 12; it is further listed as "KA THEOL. ord. 3."

Unfortunately the fragment is not in good condition; the parchment is extremely dry, discolored, and darkened to a brownish shade; the edges are curled and darkened as if the fragment has been subjected to fire damage. What appears to be a provincial notation ("Westergott. 1589 No. 12") in heavy ink in a later hand on the back of the manuscript further obscures some of the text. In spite of these blemishes, the text, in black lettering faded to brown, is largely legible. There are blue and red capitals, and the large initial "D," occupying the space of three lines, is in blue and gold with red fleuronnés;

---

[1]Schmid, p. 7.

the initial is distinguished not only by its size but also by its beautiful decorations. The red rubrics, though faded to orange, are still visible. The folio which contains the Easter material is marred by a hole just following the words *Tunc intrant presbyteri.* The folio size is 21 x 15.75 cm.

This *Visitatio sepulchri* is not represented by a full text but only contains incipits for the various items of the liturgical drama; surrounding it are incipits for psalms, antiphons, and responsories which thus embed the drama within the context of the regular Matins service for Easter morning. The *Visitatio,* which is closely related to the texts of other Type I examples from Northern Europe, ends with the office antiphon *Surrexit Dominus* and the *Te Deum.* The use of the *Surrexit Dominus* in this position is most common in the German *Visitatio,* as Susan Rankin has noted,[2] and the use of the antiphon *Maria Magdalena,* which elsewhere (in No. 5) takes a German melody, also signifies possible German influence.[3] The practice of giving merely the incipits is a usual one for this type of book, an *ordinarium* or ordinal, which is designed to give only the opening words for each item as an indication to the participants of the order of the service.[4] There is no musical notation.

Walther Lipphardt has numbered this item No. 446 (Link[1]).

---

[2]Susan Rankin, "The Music of the Medieval Liturgical Drama in France and England," Ph.D. diss. (Univ. of Cambridge, 1982), p. 136.

[3]Ibid., p. 127.

[4]Andrew Hughes, *Medieval Manuscripts for Mass and Office* (Toronto: Univ. of Toronto Press, 1982), p. 118.

<VISITATIO SEPULCHRI>

Dominica in resurrexione ad mat*utinas*

[*Antiphona.*] domine labia mea [aperies et os meum adnuntiabit laudem tuam.[1]]

[*Introitus.*] D*eus* in adiutorium [meum intende
Domine ad adiuvandum me festina:
confundantur et revereantur
qui quaerunt animam meam.[2]
Gloria Patri, et Filio, et Spiritui Sancto. Sicut erat in principio, et nunc, et semper, et in saecula saeculorum. Amen[3]].

Invit*atorium* al*leluia* al*leluia* al<*leluia*>

p*salmus* [94.] Venite [exultemus Domino
iubilemus Deo salutari nostro
praeoccupemus faciem eius in confessione
et in psalmis iubilemus ei
quoniam Deus magnus Dominus
et rex magnus super omnes deos
quia in manu eius fines terrae
et altitudines montium ipsius sunt
quoniam ipsius est mare et ipse fecit illud
et siccam manus eius formaverunt
venite adoremus et procidamus
et ploremus ante Dominum qui fecit nos
quia ipse est Deus noster
et nos populus pascuae eius
et oves manus eius

---

[1]Expansion of incipit of *Domine labia* from BSV (*Psalm* 50.17) (CAO 2355); for music, see AM 352.

[2]Expansion of incipit of *Deus in adiutorium* from BSV (*Psalm* 69.2-3); for music see LU 1027-28.

[3]*Gloria Patri* from LU 311. Lipphardt omits everything from *Deus in adiutorium* through *Angelus Domini locutus.*

hodie si vocem eius audieritis
nolite obdurare corda vestra
sicut in inritatione
secundum diem temptationis in deserto
ubi temptaverunt me patres vestri
probaverunt me: et viderunt opera mea
quadraginta annis offensus fui generationi illi
et dixi semper errant corde
et isti non cognoverunt vias meas
ut iuravi in ira mea
si intrabunt in requiem meam[4]].

In *primo* n*octurno*

*a*ntiphona. Ego sum [qui sum et consilium meum non est cum impijs. sed in lege domini voluntas mea est alleluia[5]].

p*salmus* [1.] Beat*us* uir [qui non abiit in consilio impiorum
et in via peccatorum non stetit
et in cathedra pestilentiae non sedit
sed in lege Domini voluntas eius
et in lege eius meditabitur die ac nocte
et erit tanquam lignum
quod plantatum est secus decursus aquarum
quod fructum suum dabit in tempore suo
et folium eius non defluet
et omnia quaecumque faciet prosperabuntur
non sic impii non sic:
sed tanquam pulvis quem proicit ventus a facie terrae:
ideo non resurgent impii in iudicio
neque peccatores in concilio iustorum

---

[4]Expansion of *Psalm* 94 from BSV.
[5]Expansion of incipit of *Ego sum* from BrL II, Pt. 2, 374 (CAO 2599); for music,
see LC Q1^v-Q2^r; cf. AS III, 235. The text *Ego sum qui sum* . . . is a paraphrase of
the first part of *Exodus* 3.14: *dixit Deus ad Mosen ego sum qui sum* . . . as well
as of a portion of *Psalm* 1.1: . . . *qui non abiit in consilio impiorum* . . . and of
Psalm 1.2: . . . *sed in lege Domini voluntas eius.* . . .

quoniam novit Dominus viam iustorum
et iter impiorum peribit[6]].

antiphona. Postulaui [patrem meum alleluia. dedit mihi gentes
alleluia in hereditatem alleluia[7]].

p*salmus* [2.] *Quare fremuerunt* [gentes
et populi meditati sunt inania
adstiterunt reges terrae
et principes convenerunt in unum
adversus Dominum et adversus christum eius
disrumpamus vincula eorum
et proiciamus a nobis iugum ipsorum
qui habitat in caelis inridebit eos
et Dominus subsannabit eos
tunc loquetur ad eos in ira sua
et in furore suo conturbabit eos
ego autem constitutus sum rex ab eo
super Sion montem sanctum eius
praedicans praeceptum eius
Dominus dixit ad me filius meus es tu
ego hodie genui te
postula a me et dabo tibi gentes hereditatem tuam
et possessionem tuam terminos terrae
reges eos in virga ferrea
tamquam vas figuli confringes eos
et nunc reges intellegite
erudimini qui iudicatis terram
servite Domino in timore
et exultate ei in tremore
adprehendite disciplinam
nequando irascatur Dominus et pereatis de via iusta

---

[6]Expansion of incipit of *Psalm* 1 from BSV.
[7]Expansion of incipit of *Postulaui* from BrL II, Pt. 2, 374 (CAO 4342); for music,
see LC Q2[r]. The text is a paraphrase of a portion of *Psalm* 2.8: *postula a me et
dabo tibi gentes hereditatem tuam.*

cum exarserit in brevi ira eius
beati omnes qui confidunt in eo[8]].

antiphona. Ego dormiui [et somnum cepi et exurrexi quia dominus suscepit me alleluia alleluia[9]].

psalmus [3.] Domine quid [multiplicati sunt qui tribulant me
multi insurgunt adversum me
multi dicunt animae meae
non est salus ipsi in Deo eius:
tu autem Domine susceptor meus es
gloria mea et exaltans caput meum
voce mea ad Dominum clamavi
et exaudivit me de monte sancto suo
ego dormivi et soporatus sum
exsurrexi quia Dominus suscipiet me
non timebo milia populi circumdantis me
exsurge Domine salvum me fac Deus meus
quoniam tu percussisti omnes adversantes mihi sine causa
dentes peccatorum contrivisti
Domini est salus et super populum tuum benedictio tua[10]].

versus.[11] Quem queris mulier [alleluia.
Responsorium. Uiuentem cum mortuis alleluia.[12]]

---

[8]Expansion of *Psalm* 2 from BSV.

[9]Expansion of incipit of *Ego dormiui* from BrL II, Pt. 2, 374 (variant of CAO 2572); for music, see LC Q2^v (variant text); cf. AS III, 235. The text is a paraphrase of *Psalm* 3.6: *ego dormivi et soporatus sum / exsurrexi quia Dominus suscipiet me.*

[10]Expansion of *Psalm* 3 from BSV.

[11]This item should properly be designated as a *responsorium*; see John Bryden and David G. Hughes, *An Index of Gregorian Chant* (Cambridge: Harvard Univ. Press, 1969), I, 344.

[12]Expansion of incipit of *Quem queris* from BrL II, Pt. 2, 374 (CAO 7468); for musical setting, see WA 145.

eu*angeliu*m marci[13]

[IN illo tempore.[14]] [*Antiphon*.] Maria magd*alena* [et maria iacobi et salome emerunt aromata: vt venientes vngerent iesum. . .[15]].

<cum exp*ositione gregorii*>[16]
[*Gregorij pape*. Audistis fratres charissimi quod sancte mulieres que dominum secute fuerant cum aromatibus ad monumentum venerunt: vt eum quem viuentem dilexerant etiam mortuo studio humanitatis obsequuntur.[17]]

Responsorium. Angel*us* do*mini* [descendit de celo et accedens reuoluit lapidem et super eum sedit et dixit mulieribus nolite timere scio enim quia crucifixum queritis. Jam surrexit venite et videte locum vbi positus erat dominus alleluia.
Versus. Angelus domini locutus est mulieribus dicens quem queritis an iesum queritis. Jam *surrexit venite et videte locum vbi positus erat dominus alleluia*.[18]]

[*Lectio ij*. Sed res gesta aliud in sancta ecclesia significat gerendum. Sic quippe necesse est vt audiamus que facta sunt: quatinus cogitemus etiam que nobis sunt ex eorum imitatione facienda. Et

---

[13]The Lesson: *Mark* 16. For this rubric as it appears in No. 4, below, see Sven Helander, *Ordinarius Lincopensis ca. 1400 och dess liturgiska förebilder* (Uppsala: Almqvist & Wiksell, 1957), p. 335.

[14]BrL II, Pt. 2, 375 (incipit of Lesson I).

[15]Expansion of incipit of *Maria Magdalena* from BrL II, Pt. 2, 375. The expansion of the incipit in this case is consistent also with CAO 3702 (*Maria Magdalena et Maria Jacobi et Salome emerunt aromata, ut venientes ungerent Jesum, alleluia*) rather than CAO 7128 (*Maria Magdalena et altera Maria ibant diluculo ad monumentum . . .*). For the completion of the Gospel reading, see *Mark* 16.2-8.

[16]The Homily of St. Gregory. For the rubric as it appears in No. 4, below, see Helander, p. 335.

[17]BrL II, Pt. 2, 375; a full translation of this homily as it appears in the liturgy will be found in Prosper Guéranger, *The Liturgical Year*, trans. Laurence Shepherd (Westminster, Maryland: Newman Press, 1949), pp. 118-21.

[18]Expansion of the incipit of *Angelus Domini* from BrL II, Pt. 2, 375 (CAO 6093); for music, see LC Q2[v]-Q3[v]; cf. AS III, 235-36.

nos igitur in eum qui mortuus est credentes: si odore virtutum refecti cum opinione bonorum operum dominum querimus: ad monumentum profecto illius cum aromatibus venimus.[19]]

Responsorium. angelus [domini locutus est cum mulieribus dicens quem queritis an iesum queritis. Jam surrexit venite et videte alleluia alleluia.
Versus. Ecce precedet vos in galyleam ibi eum videbitis sicut dixit vobis. Jam *surrexit venite et videte alleluia alleluia*[20]].

[*Lectio iij.* Ille autem mulieres angelos vident que cum aromatibus venerunt: quia videlicet ille mentes supernos ciues aspiciunt que cum virtutum odoribus ad deum per sancta desideria profiscuntur. . . .[21]]

Responsorium. Dum trans*isset* [sabbatum maria magdalene et maria iacobi et salome emerunt aromata. Ut venientes vngerent iesum alleluia alleluia[22]].

<*versus.* Et valde> [mane vna sabbatorum veniunt ad monumentum orto iam sole. Ut *venientes vngerent iesum alleluia alleluia.*[23] Gloria *Patri, et Filio, et Spiritui Sancto. Sicut erat in principio, et nunc, et semper, et in saecula saeculorum. Amen*[24]].

Responsorium iteru*m.* Dum transisset [sabbatum maria magdalena et maria iacobi et salome emerunt aromata. Ut venientes vngerent iesum alleluia alleluia].

---

[19]BrL II, Pt. 2, 375.
[20]Expansion of incipit of *Angelus Domini* from BrL II, Pt. 2, 375 (CAO 6095); for music, see LC Q3ᵛ-Q4ʳ; cf. AS III, 236.
[21]BrL II, Pt. 2, 375.
[22]Expansion of incipit of *Dum transisset* from BrL II, Pt. 2, 375 (CAO 6565); for music, see LC Q4ᵛ-R1ʳ; cf. AS III, 236-37. This chant is listed by Bryden and Hughes as *Cum transisset* in their *Index of Gregorian Chant*, pp. 103, 142.
[23]BrL II, Pt. 2, 375; for music see LC R1ʳ; cf. AS III, 237 (CAO 6565).
[24]*Gloria Patri* from LU 311.

Sic <cantantes *procedunt*> ad sepulchr*um et* stant foris expectantes et <tres>[25] p*resbite*ri p*ro* mulier*ibus* in capis ueniunt <cum> thurribulis *et* duo diaconi sedent int*us* cu*m* dal<maticis> p*ro* Angelis *et* sic incipiu*nt* p*resbite*ri.

Quis reuol<uet nobis ab hostio lapidem>

Respondent diaconi.

Quem que<ritis> in sepulchrum

p*resbite*ri

Ih*esu*m nazarenum.

Respondent <diaconi>

Non *est* hic sed surexit.

et addunt.

Venite <*et* uidete> [locum, ubi positus erat Dominus, Alleluia[26]].

Tunc intrant p*resbite*ri thurrificantes <lo>cum *et* addunt diaconi.

[*antiphona*.] Cito euntes [dicite discipulis eius et petro quia surrexit dominus alleluia[27]].

et tollunt <Marie>[28] lintheamina *et* p*ro*cedu*nt* ad p*opulum* cantantes.

---

[25]Lipphardt: ecce.
[26]Expansion of incipit of *Venite et videte* from LC Q3^r-Q3^v (CAO 5352).
[27]Expansion of *Cito euntes* from BrL II, Pt. 2, 390; cf. AS III, 250, WA 129 (variant of CAO 1813).
[28]Lipphardt, Schmid: presbiteri.

Surrexit *dominus* de sepulcro [alleluia. Qui pro nobis pependit in ligno alleluia[29]].

Tunc cantor incipit.

Te *deum* laudam*us* [te Dominum confitemur.
Te aeternum Patrem omnis terra veneratur.
Tibi omnes Angeli, tibi Caeli et universae Potestates:
Tibi Cherubim et Seraphim incessabili voce proclamant:
Sanctus: Sanctus: Sanctus Dominus Deus Sabaoth.
Pleni sunt caeli et terra majestatis gloriae tuae.
Te gloriosus Apostolorum chorus:
Te Prophetarum laudabilis numerus:
Te Martyrum candidatus laudat exercitus.
Te per orbem terrarum sancta confitetur Ecclesia:
Patrem immensae majestatis:
Venerandum tuum verum, et unicum Filium:
Sanctum quoque Paraclitum Spiritum.
Tu Rex gloriae, Christe.
Tu Patris sempiternus es Filius.
Tu ad liberandum suscepturus hominem,
non horruisti Virginis uterum.
Tu devicto mortis aculeo, aperuisti credentibus regna caelorum.
Tu ad dexteram Dei sedes, in gloria Patris.
Judex crederis esse venturus.
Te ergo quaesumus, tuis famulis subveni, quos pretioso sanguine redemisti.
Aeterna fac cum Sanctis tuis in gloria numerari.
Salvum fac populum tuum Domine, et benedic hereditati tuae.
Et rege eos, et extolle illos usque in aeternum.
Per singulos dies, benedicimus te.
Et laudamus nomen tuum in saeculorum, et in saeculum saeculi.
Dignare Domine die isto sine peccato nos custodire.
Miserere nostri Domine, miserere nostri.

---

[29]Expansion of incipit of *Surrexit Domini* from BrL II, Pt. 2, 389 (CAO 7739); for music see AS III, 250; cf. LU 239.

Fiat misericordia tua Domine super nos, quemadmodum speravimus in te.

In te Domine speravi: non confundar in aeternum[30]].

conpulsatis iterum *omnibus* signis. postea <non> dice*tur* *uer*sus ne*que* d*eus* in adiutoriu*m* sed statim. a*ntiphona* ad laud*es.*

Angel*us* [autem domini descendit de celo et accedens reuoluit lapidem et sedebat super eum alleluia alleluia[31]].

THE VISIT TO THE SEPULCHER

Sunday of the Resurrection at Matins

Antiphon. Lord, open my lips, and my mouth shall show forth your praise.

Introit. O God, make speed to save me: O Lord, make haste to help me. Let them be confounded and put to shame who seek after my soul. Glory to the Father and to the Son and to the Holy Spirit. As it was in the beginning, is now, and ever shall be, world without end. Amen.

Invitatory. Alleluia, alleluia, alleluia.

Psalm 94. Come, let us praise the Lord with joy:
let us joyfully sing to God our savior.
Let us come before his presence with thanksgiving;
and make a joyful noise to him with psalms.
For the Lord is a great God,
and a great king above all gods.

---

[30]Expansion of incipit of *Te Deum* from LU 1832-34.
[31]Expansion of incipit of *Angelus autem Domini* from BrL II, Pt. 2, 376; for music see LC R1ᵛ; cf. AS III, 237 (CAO 1408).

For in his hand are all the ends of the earth:
and the heights of the mountains are his.
For the sea is his, and he made it:
and his hands formed the dry land.
Come, let us adore and fall down:
and weep before the Lord that made us.
For he is the Lord our God:
and we are the sheep of his pasture and the sheep of his hand.
Today if you shall hear his voice,
harden not your hearts:
As in the provocation, according to the day of temptation in the wilderness:
where your fathers tempted me, they proved me, and saw my works.
Forty years long was I offended with that generation, and I said:
These always err in heart.
And these men have not known my ways:
so I swore in my wrath that they shall not enter into my rest.

At the first nocturn.

Antiphon. I am who am, and my counsel is not with the ungodly: but my delight is in the law of the Lord, alleluia.

Psalm 1. Blessed is the man who has not walked in the counsel of the ungodly,
nor stood in the way of sinners, nor sat in the chair of pestilence.
But his will is in the law of the Lord,
and on his law he shall meditate day and night.
And he shall be like a tree which is planted near the running waters,
which shall bring forth its fruit, in due season.
And his leaf shall not fall off:
and all whatsoever he shall do shall prosper.
Not so the wicked, not so:
but they are like the dust, which the wind drives from the face of the earth.

Therefore the wicked shall not rise again in judgment:
nor sinners in the council of the just.
For the Lord knows the way of the just:
and the way of the wicked shall perish.

Antiphon. I have asked my father, alleluia, and he has given me
the nations, alleluia.

Psalm 2. Why have the Gentiles raged,
and the people devised vain things?
The kings of the earth stood up, and the princes met together,
against the Lord, and against his Christ.
Let us break their bonds asunder:
and let us cast away their yoke from us.
He that dwells in heaven shall laugh at them:
and the Lord shall deride them.
Then shall he speak to them in his anger,
and trouble them in his rage.
But I am appointed king by him over Sion his holy mountain,
preaching his commandment.
The Lord has said to me: You are my son,
this day have I begotten you.
Ask of me, and I will give you the Gentiles for your inheritance,
And the utmost parts of the earth for your possession.
You shall rule them with a rod of iron,
and shall break them in pieces like a potter's vessel.
And now, O you kings, understand:
receive instruction, you that judge the earth.
Serve you the Lord with fear:
and rejoice unto him with trembling.
Embrace discipline, lest at any time the Lord be angry,
and you perish from the just way.
When his wrath shall be kindled in a short time,
blessed are all they that trust in him.

Antiphon. I have slept and have taken my rest, and I have risen
up again because the Lord sustained me, alleluia, alleluia.

Psalm 3. Why, O Lord, are they multiplied that afflict me?
many are they who rise up against me.
Many say to my soul:
There is no salvation for him in his God.
But you, O Lord, are my protector,
my glory, and the lifter up of my head.
I have cried to the Lord with my voice:
and he has heard me from his holy hill.
I have slept and have taken my rest:
and I have risen up, because the Lord has protected me.
I will not fear thousands of the people, surrounding me:
arise, O Lord; save me, O my God.
For you have struck all them who are my adversaries without cause:
you have broken the teeth of sinners.
Salvation is of the Lord:
and your blessing is upon your people.

Verse. Whom do you seek, woman? Alleluia, alleluia.

Responsory. I seek the living among the dead.

The Gospel according to Mark.

Antiphon. Mary Magdalene and Mary Jacobi and Salome bought spices, seeking to anoint the Lord. . . .

With commentary by Gregory.
Pope Gregory. [*Lesson I.*] You have heard, dearly beloved brothers, how the holy women who had followed the Lord came with spices to the tomb, and how, since they loved him when he was alive, they planned to honor him, now that he had died, with proofs of their love.

Responsory. The angel of the Lord came down from heaven, and as he came closer, he rolled away the stone and sat upon it. And he said to the women, "Fear not. I know that you seek the crucified one. He is risen. Come and see the place where the Lord was laid, alleluia."

Verse. The angel of the Lord spoke to the women and said, "Whom do you seek? Is it not Jesus you seek? He is risen. Come and see the place where the Lord was laid, alleluia."

Lesson II. But this that they did signifies what the members of the holy Church should be doing. We must listen to what was done so that we may learn what to do to imitate those things. And we who believe in him who has died, if we are characterized by the good odor of virtue and by a reputation for good works, may be said to come to the sepulcher with sweet spices.

Responsory. The angel of the Lord spoke to the women and said, "Whom do you seek? Is it not Jesus you seek? He is risen. Come and see, alleluia, alleluia."
Verse. Behold, he goes before you into Galilee where you will see him, as he said. He is risen. Come and see, alleluia, alleluia.

Lesson III. However, the women who had brought spices saw the angels; thus souls, fragrant in their virtue, come to the vision of the celestial citizens as they are drawn toward the Lord by their holy desires. . . .

Responsory. When the sabbath had ended, Mary Magdalene and Mary the mother of James and Salome bought spices and came to anoint Jesus, alleluia, alleluia.

Verse. And indeed, early one sabbath morning they came to the grave at the rising of the sun and came to anoint Jesus, alleluia, alleluia. Glory to the Father and to the Son and to the Holy Spirit. As it was in the beginning, is now, and ever shall be, world without end. Amen.

Responsory (repeated). When the sabbath had ended, Mary Magdalene and Mary the mother of James and Salome bought spices and came to anoint Jesus, alleluia, alleluia.

So singing, they proceed to the tomb, and standing outside they wait, and three priests in copes, taking the women's roles, arrive with thuribles, and two deacons in dalmatics, taking the angels' roles, are seated inside, and the priests [impersonating the Marys] begin like this:

"Who will roll the stone away from the door for us?"

The deacons reply:

"Whom do you seek in the sepulcher?"

Priests:

"Jesus of Nazareth."

The deacons reply:

"He is not here, but is risen."

And add:

"Come and see the place where the Lord was laid, alleluia."

Then the priests enter and cense the place, and the deacons add:

Antiphon. Go quickly and tell the disciples and Peter that the Lord is risen, alleluia.

And the Marys pick up their linen cloths and proceed toward the people singing,

"The Lord, who for our sake hung upon the tree, is risen from the tomb. Alleluia, alleluia, alleluia."

Then the cantor intones:

We praise you, God: we acknowledge you to be the Lord.

You are the eternal Father: the whole world worships you.

To you all the angels, the heavens, and all the Powers, Cherubim and Seraphim, proclaim aloud unceasingly,

"Holy, holy, holy Lord, God of Sabaoth.

Heaven and earth are full of the majesty of your glory."

The glorious company of the apostles, the laudable host of prophets, the white-clad band of martyrs praise you.

The holy Church throughout the whole earth confesses that you are the Father of unlimited majesty; true and worthy of honor, your only Son; also the holy Spirit, the comforter.

You are the king of glory, O Christ. You are the eternal Son of the Father.

When you came to liberate humans, you did not scorn the Virgin's womb.

You overcame the sting of Death: you opened the kingdom of heaven to all believers.

You are seated at the right hand of God, in the glory of the Father: we believe that you will come to be our judge.

We therefore ask that you come and help your people, whom you have redeemed with your precious blood.

Cause them to be counted with your saints in eternal glory.

Save your people, Lord, and bless your inheritance.

Rule them, and raise them up in eternity.

Daily we bless you and we praise your name, world without end.

Keep us, Lord, this day without sin.

Have mercy on us, Lord, have mercy on us.

Let your mercy, Lord, be upon us, as we have trusted in you.

In you, Lord, have I trusted. I will never be confounded.

Anew, with all the bells ringing together, thereafter the verse "O God, make speed" is not heard, but immediately the antiphon for Lauds [is sung]:

The angel of the Lord came down from heaven, and came forth and rolled away the stone, and sat upon it. Alleluia, alleluia.

2

Visitatio Sepulchri
from a Linköping Antiphonal

A second Type I *Visitatio sepulchri* is contained in a fragment of a thirteenth-century Antiphonal from Linköping (Riksarkivet, Småland 1574, No. 3:2).[1] The only vestiges remaining of the Matins service to which this *Visitatio* must have belonged are Psalm 94 (identified by the incipit only), the antiphon *Dum transisset sabbatum*, and the *Te Deum* (also indicated only by its incipit), the latter ending the service. The inclusion of a *Visitatio* in an antiphonal, although rare, would have been quite appropriate, since this type of service book contained necessary music for the Office, including invitatories, antiphons, hymns, and responsories.[2]

The fragment consists of two parchment folios with both text and music, in square notation on a four-line staff; one of the four pages is barely legible and presumably has been darkened by fire. The long, thin initials with distinctive horizontal and diagonal cross-barring are red and black, and the rubrics are red. The leaf which contains the pertinent Easter Matins and *Visitatio sepulchri* measures 37.25 x 20.5 cm. un-

---

[1]Identified by Schmid, pp. 2-4, and Lipphardt as Vitterhetsakademien, Cod. Fragm., Ant. 132.
[2]Hughes, *Medieval Manuscripts for Mass and Office*, p. 119.

folded; 34 x 20.5 cm. with top folded; and 30 x 20.5 with top and bottom folded.

Attached to a set of provincial records from Småland, the *Visitatio* appears on the page that serves as the inside front cover of the collection; it is placed upside down on the records. The damage to the fragment over time is serious and has rendered portions of text and music illegible. The parchment is dry and wrinkled and has been harmed further by being carelessly attached to the records. The folios have been turned under at the edges and sewn or tied to the records; thus, some of the notation with the essential clefs also is not readily accessible, though it is possible to see the clefs by careful examination of the fragment. Unfortunately, the strings that bind the fragment to the records are now tearing the parchment so that it is currently at great danger and risk. Better conservation of this fragment is urgently needed.

The use of *o celicole* in the address to the angels is normally found in ceremonies included in a group found in the region near the Rhine in modern Germany,[3] and hence argues here for influence on this Swedish ceremony from those areas.

Lipphardt's edition of the text appears under the number 448 (Link[3]).

---

[3]Rankin, "The Music of the Medieval Liturgical Drama," p. 25; Helmut de Boor, *Die Textgeschichte der Lateinischen Osterfeiern* (Tübingen: Max Niemeyer, 1967), pp. 67-68.

\<VISITATIO SEPULCHRI\>

uenite et uidete [locum, ubi positus erat Dominus[1]] alleluia alleluia.

\<Ihe\>sum[2] queritis \< . . . \>

\< . . . \> no\<n\> est hic[3]

[*Psalmus 94.*] Venite [exultemus Domino
iubilemus Deo salutari nostro
praeoccupemus faciem eius in confessione
et in psalmis iubilemus ei
quoniam Deus magnus Dominus
et rex magnus super omnes deos
quia in manu eius fines terrae
et altitudines montium ipsius sunt
quoniam ipsius est mare et ipse fecit illud
et siccam manus eius formaverunt
venite adoremus et procidamus
et ploremus ante Dominum qui fecit nos
quia ipse est Deus noster
et nos populus pascuae eius
et oves manus eius
hodie si vocem eius audieritis
nolite obdurare corda vestra
sicut in inritatione
secundum diem temptationis in deserto
ubi temptaverunt me patres vestri
probaverunt me: et viderunt opera mea
quadraginta annis offensus fui generationi illi
et dixi semper errant corde
et isti non cognoverunt vias meas

---

[1]Expansion of incipit of *Venite et uidete* from LC Q3ʳ-Q3ᵛ; cf. AS III, 236 (CAO 5352).
[2]Lipphardt: Jesum.
[3]Lipphardt omits *Non est hic* and the incipit to *Psalm* 94.

ut iuravi in ira mea
si intrabunt in requiem meam[4]].

Responsorium. Dum transisset sabba<tum> <maria> <mag-d>alena et maria iacobi et salomee emerunt aromata ut ue<-nientes vngerent> iesum alleluia alleluia.[5]

Versus. Et ualde <m>ane una sabbatorum ueniunt ad monu-mentum orto iam so<le ut uenien>tes [vngerent iesum alleluia al-leluia].[6] Gloria [Patri et Filio, et Spiritui Sancto. Sicut erat in principio, et nunc, et semper, et in saecula saeculorum. Amen[7]].

[*Responsorium.*] Dum transisset [sabbatum maria magdalena et maria iacobi et salomee emerunt aromata ut uenientes ungerent iesum alleluia alleluia].

Sic cantantes procedunt ad sepulcrum et stant foris expectantes. et ecce tres clericj pro mulieribus in cappis ueniunt ad sepulcrum. cum turribulis sedentibus intro duobus diaconibus cum dalmaticis pro angelis. et sic incipient extra stantes

<Quis reuolu>et nobis lapidem ab <hostio[8] monu>menti alleluia alleluia.

Quem queritis in sepulchro o christicole.

Item extra stan⌈tes⌉

Ihe<sum nazarenum> o celicole.

<De>intus sedentes respondent

---

[4]Expansion of Psalm 94 from BSV.
[5]Cf. BrL II, Pt. 2, 375; LC Q4ᵛ-R1ʳ; AS III, 236-37 (CAO 6565).
[6]Cf. BrL II, Pt. 2, 375; LC R1ʳ; AS III, 237 (CAO 6565).
[7]For *Gloria Patri*, see LU 311.
[8]Lipphardt: ostio.

Non est hic surrexit enim sicut predixerat ite <nunciate quia> surrexit iesus.

Et addunt

Uenite et uidete locum ubi positus erat do<minus alleluia> alleluia.

Tunc intrant turificantes locum.

<et> addunt angeli.

[*Antiphona.*] Cito euntes dicite discipulis qui<a s>urrexit <dominus alleluia> *in secvlorum amen.*[9]

Et tollunt marie lintheamina procedunt ad populum cantantes.

Surrexit dominus de sepulchro qui <pro nobis pependit> in ligno. alleluia alleluia.[10]

Tunc cantor incipit. te deum.

Te deum [laudamus: te Dominum confitemur.
Te aeternum Patrem onmis terra veneratur.
Tibi omnes Angeli, tibi Caeli et universae Potestates:
Tibi Cherubim et Seraphim incessabili voce proclamant:
Sanctus: Sanctus: Sanctus Dominus Deus Sabaoth.
Pleni sunt caeli et terra majestatis gloriae tuae.
Te gloriosus Apostolorum chorus:
Te Prophetarum laudabilis numerus:
Te Martyrum candidatus laudat exercitus.
Te per orbem terrarum sancta confitetur Ecclesia:

---

[9]Cf. AS III, 250 (CAO 1813); Schmid and Lipphardt: omit e v o u ae.
[10]Cf. BrL II, Pt. 2, 389; AS III, 250 (CAO 7739). On the music of this item, see also Clyde W. Brockett, "The Role of the Office Antiphon," *Musica Disciplina*, 34 (1980), 17.

Patrem immensae majestatis:
Venerandum tuum verum, et unicum Filium:
Sanctum quoque Paraclitum Spiritum.
Tu Rex gloriae, Christe.
Tu Patris sempiternus es Filius.
Tu ad liberandum suscepturus hominem,
non horruisti Virginis uterum.
Tu devicto mortis aculeo, aperuisti credentibus regna caelorum.
Tu ad dexteram Dei sedes, in gloria Patris.
Judex crederis esse venturus.
Te ergo quaesumus, tuis famulis subveni, quos pretioso sanguine redemisti.
Aeterna fac cum Sanctis tuis in gloria numerari.
Salvum fac populum tuum Domine, et benedic hereditati tuae.
Et rege eos, et extolle illos usque in aeternum.
Per singulos dies, benedicimus te.
Et laudamus nomen tuum in saeculorum, et in saeculum saeculi.
Dignare Domine die isto sine peccato nos custodire.
Miserere nostri Domine, miserere nostri.
Fiat misericordia tua Domine super nos, quemadmodum speravimus in te.
In te Domine speravi: non confundar in aeternum[11]].

Postea non dicetur versus neque deus in adiutorium sed statim antiphon.

<Angelus> dominj descendit de celo et accedens reuoluit lapidem et se | <debat> [super eum alleluia alleluia[12]].

---

[11]Expansion of incipit of *Te Deum* from LU 1832-34.
[12]Expansion of incipit of *Angelus Dominj* from BrL II, Pt. 2, 376; cf. CAO 1408: *Angelus autem Domini descendit de coelo, et accedens revolvit lapidem, et sedebat super eum, alleluia alleluia.*

THE VISIT TO THE SEPULCHER

Come and see the place where the Lord was laid. Alleluia, alleluia.

You seek Jesus. . . .

. . . He is not here.

Psalm 94. Come, let us praise the Lord with joy:
let us joyfully sing to God our savior.
Let us come before his presence with thanksgiving;
and make a joyful noise to him with psalms.
For the Lord is a great God,
and a great king above all gods.
For in his hand are all the ends of the earth:
and the heights of the mountains are his.
For the sea is his, and he made it:
and his hands formed the dry land.
Come, let us adore and fall down:
and weep before the Lord that made us.
For he is the Lord our God:
and we are the people of his pasture and the sheep of his hand.
Today if you shall hear his voice,
harden not your hearts:
As in the provocation, according to the day of temptation in the wilderness:
Where your fathers tempted me, they proved me, and saw my works.
Forty years long was I offended with that generation, and I said:
These always err in heart.
And these men have not known my ways:
so I swore in my wrath that they shall not enter into my rest.

Responsory. When the sabbath had ended, Mary Magdalene and Mary the mother of James and Salome bought spices and came to anoint Jesus. Alleluia, alleluia.

Verse. And indeed, early one sabbath morning they came to the grave as at the rising of the sun and came to anoint Jesus. Alleluia, alleluia. Glory to the Father and to the Son and to the holy Spirit. As it was in the beginning, is now, and ever shall be, world without end. Amen.

Responsory. When the sabbath had ended, Mary Magdalene and Mary the mother of James and Salome bought spices and came to anoint Jesus. Alleluia, alleluia.

So singing, they proceed to the tomb, and, standing outside, they wait; and three priests in copes, taking the women's parts, arrive at the sepulcher with thuribles, and two deacons in dalmatics, taking the angels' parts, are seated inside, and those standing outside begin thus:

"Who will roll the stone away from the door of the tomb for us? Alleluia, alleluia."

"Whom do you seek in the sepulcher, O Christians?"

Again, those standing outside:

"Jesus of Nazareth, O heavenly ones."

Those seated inside reply:

"He is not here but is risen, just as he said. Go and tell the others that Jesus is risen."

And they add:

"Come and see the place where the Lord was laid. Alleluia, alleluia."

Then they enter and cense the place.
And the angels add:

Antiphon. "Go quickly and tell the disciples that the Lord is risen. Alleluia, world without end, Amen."

And the Marys pick up the linens and proceed toward the people, singing:

"The Lord, who for our sake hung upon the tree, is risen from the grave. Alleluia, alleluia."

Then the cantor intones the Te Deum:

We praise you, God: we acknowledge you to be the Lord.
You are the eternal Father: the whole world worships you.
To you all the angels, the heavens, and all the Powers, Cherubim and Seraphim, proclaim aloud unceasingly,
"Holy, holy, holy, Lord God of Sabaoth.
Heaven and earth are full of the majesty of your glory."
The glorious company of the apostles, the laudable host of prophets, the white-clad band of martyrs praise you.
The holy Church throughout the whole earth confesses that you are the Father of unlimited majesty; true and worthy of honor, your only Son; also the holy Spirit, the comforter.
You are the king of glory, O Christ. You are the eternal Son of the Father.
When you came to liberate humans, you did not scorn the Virgin's womb.
You overcame the sting of Death: you opened the kingdom of heaven to all believers.
You are seated at the right hand of God, in the glory of the Father: we believe that you will come to be our judge.
We therefore ask that you come and help your people, whom you have redeemed with your precious blood.
Cause them to be counted with your saints in eternal glory.
Save your people, Lord, and bless your inheritance.
Rule them, and raise them up in eternity.
Daily we bless you, and we praise your name, world without end.
Keep us, Lord, this day without sin.

Have mercy on us, Lord, have mercy on us.
Let your mercy, Lord, be upon us, as we have trusted in you.
In you, Lord, have I trusted. I will never be confounded.

Following the Te Deum, *"O God, make speed" is not said, but the antiphon follows immediately:*

The angel of the Lord came down from heaven, and came and rolled away the stone, and sat upon it. Alleluia, alleluia.

3

Visitatio Sepulchri
from a Gradual
Possibly from the Stockholm Area

A brief *Visitatio sepulchri* is contained in one of the fragments of a thirteenth-century Gradual identified as such by Toni Schmid[1] and currently at Riksarkivet in Stockholm. The fragment which contains the Easter ceremony appears under the shelfmark Dalarna 1575, No. 14. The Gradual comes from an as yet undetermined Swedish church, perhaps near Stockholm. The *Visitatio* retains the Anglo-Norman *o celicole* used with reference to the angels. Schmid notes that the fragment contains the first eight lines for a hymn to the Holy Spirit; the hymn is completed in another fragment from the same Gradual.[2] She also indicates that the Gradual interestingly contains hymn sequences—e.g., the "Olafsequence" (*Lux illuxit letabunda*)—which come from St. Martial in Limoges as well as a hymn, *Ardua spes mundi*, from St. Gall, indicating a French origin.[3]

The folio which contains the *Visitatio* measures 20.5 x 14

---

[1]Schmid, pp. 2-4, 8-10.
[2]Ibid., pp. 8-10. The hymn is completed in Vitterhetsakademien, Cod. Fragm. Sequ. 136.
[3]Schmid, p. 10.

cm. and is parchment, dry and with edges singed. The single rubric (*In die pasce*) is red, while the smaller narrow capitals are black lined with red. One larger initial is red and black with blue-decorated center. At the words *Per dominum*, the black letters are lined with red. The drama, which is preceded by the incipit for a *Kyrie eleison*, is fully noted in square notation on four lines with the exception of a prayer which serves as conclusion.

The Type I *Visitatio* itself is extremely concise, consisting only of the simple question-answer exchange between angels and holy women and the antiphon *Surrexit Dominus*. There are no rubrics indicating representation of the angels or holy women, nor are there directions as to how the passages are to be sung (e.g., *submissa voce*). Thus the questions and the rejoinders outline the stark structure of this ceremony.

There is evidence of scribal carelessness. The words *o celicole*, *a morte*, and, in the prayer, *a nobis* are joined together, and the word *ligno* has been rendered as *lingo*. At *nobis*, in *Surrexit Dominus*, the first syllable is repeated, and the first attempt at *nob* is crossed out. Latin solecisms such as *reuoluat* and *predixeram* are present. In the prayer, the words *a* and *nobis* are elided. In addition to the odd orthography, the musical setting for the familiar text is unlike any of the other Swedish fragments, arguing for a scribe whose memory was faulty or who was out of touch with the rest of Swedish liturgical tradition.

Lipphardt identifies the fragment as Vitterhetsakademien Cod. Fragm. Sequ. 37, and has numbered this *Visitatio* as No. 450 (Stock[1]).

Number Three

\<VISITATIO SEPULCHRI\>

In die pasce

Qvis reuoluat[1] nobis lapidem ab ostio monu\<menti\> alleluia. alleluia.

Quem queritis in sepulcro \<o christi\>cole.

Jhesum nazarenum crucifixum ocelicole.

\<Non\> est hic surrexit sicut predixeram[2] ite nunciate \<quia\> surrexit amorte.

venite *et* uidete locum ubi \<positus\> erat dominus. Alleluia. alleluia.

Surrexit \<dominus\> de sepulchro qui´pro ~~nob~~ nobis pependit in ling\<o\>[3] \<alleluia\>.

Deus qui pro nobis filium tuum crucis patib\<ulum\> subire uoluisti. *et* inimici anobis expelleres \<potestatem\> concede nobis famulis tuis. ut in resurrectionis e\<ius gau\>diis semper uiuamus. *Per dominum nostrum ihesum* \<christum.\>[4]

---

[1]Lipphardt marks this Latin solecism with an exclamation point within brackets in his text.

[2]Lipphardt: predixerat. The MS. *predixeram* is indicated in his notes.

[3]Lipphardt: ligno. The MS. *ling[no]* (sic) is indicated in his notes.

[4]Lipphardt omits the prayer. However, it is transcribed by Schmid, who remarks that "the prayer is found as an oratio in the Mass for Wednesday in Easter week and also in the Votive Mass for the Holy Cross" (p. 12). Further, she notes, it can also be found in the Elevation of the Cross or Host on Easter morning. See additionally BrL, where it appears at Laudes on Wednesday of Holy Week (II, Pt. 2, 363) and at Laudes on Tuesday of the week following Easter day (II, Pt. 2, 393). In its unabbreviated form in the breviary the text reads: "Deus qui pro nobis filium tuum crucis patibulum subire voluisti: vt inimici a nobis expelleres potestatem: concede nobis famulis tuis: vt resurrectionis gratiam consequamur. Per eundem" (II, Pt. 2, 363).

THE VISIT TO THE SEPULCHER

On Easter Day

Who will roll the stone away from the door of the tomb for us? Alleluia, alleluia.

Whom do you seek in the sepulcher, O Christians?

Jesus of Nazareth crucified, O heavenly ones.

He is not here; he is risen as he had said he would. Go and say that he is risen from the dead.

Come and see the place where the Lord was laid. Alleluia, alleluia.

The Lord who for our sake hung upon the tree has risen from the tomb. Alleluia.

[Prayer.] O God, who for our sake was willing to submit your son to the gibbet of the cross, and who drove away from us the power of the enemy, grant that we, your servants, may always live in the joys of his resurrection. Through our Lord Jesus Christ.

4

Elevatio Crucis and *Visitatio Sepulchri*
from a Vadstena Ordinal

St. Birgitta, a patron saint of Sweden, was born about 1303 and was married in 1316 when she was around thirteen years of age; in spite of living in the secular world, she nevertheless served God through her holy life, deeds of charity, and the mystical visions which were sent to her unbidden. One of the ways in which she expressed her own piety, as lady-in-waiting to Blanche of Namur, wife of King Magnus Eriksson, was to urge the king and queen to lead lives of holiness. After Birgitta's husband died in 1344, she took on the role of penitent and mystic, being visited with visions which called the king and the Swedish people to repentance. Birgitta's criticisms of the king's life notwithstanding, in 1346 Magnus chose to endow the monastery, a double one for men and women, for Birgitta at Vadstena, thus giving her a location for establishing the Brigittine Order.

In 1349 Birgitta went to Rome in order to attempt to gain official status for the Order; this was accomplished in 1370, with the Order receiving its confirmation by Pope Urban V, although there was an agreement that the Rule was to be that of the Augustinian Order. Birgitta herself never returned to Sweden in her lifetime; after her death in

1373, her remains, to be venerated as relics, were brought back to Vadstena by her daughter, St. Catherine of Sweden. Birgitta's canonization in 1391 received its confirmation in 1415.[1]

On St. Severinus' Day (October 23) in 1384, Nicolaus Hermanni, bishop of the Linköping diocese, made a visit to Birgitta's monastery-convent and at that time instituted the use of an Ordinal from the Linköping diocese for both brothers and sisters there.[2] This Ordinal contains, as is customary, incipits for Mass and Office items for the liturgical year; included in the Ordinal (pp. hi-hii) are an *Elevatio crucis* and a *Visitatio sepulchri.*

The manuscript is in good condition. It is a quarto measuring 24 x 17 cm., and is intact as a volume bound in leather with broken clasps and with a few small wormholes in the cover. The text is in a neat and regular Gothic hand; as is usual in the case of ordinals, there are only incipits present; there is no notation. The rubrics are red, the text is black, with the one large initial, "I," being in red. Throughout the book are scattered some blue initials, but none of these are present in pages hi and hii. Wormholes in scattered leaves

---

[1] Useful brief biographies and bibliographic information concerning St. Birgitta (St. Bridget of Sweden) are contained in *The Catholic Encyclopaedia,* II, 782, *The New Catholic Encyclopedia,* II, 799, and *The Oxford Dictionary of the Christian Church,* 2nd ed., ed. F. L. Cross (Oxford: Oxford Univ. Press, 1974), p. 200. There is a popular life by Johannes Jorgensen (*Saint Bridget of Sweden,* trans. Ingeborg Lund [London: Longmans Green, 1954], 2 vols.).

[2] Helander, *Ordinarius Lincopensis,* p. 38. As Helander notes, the manuscript takes into consideration and makes reference to the Brigittine Rule. See also Schmid, "Das Osterspiel in Schweden," pp. 1, 5, who also cites a letter of 1506 from Kaplan Olauus Jacobj to Petrus Jacobi that further documents the provenance.

are found throughout the book.

The *Elevatio* text begins with *Surrexit Dominus*, and then continues with stanzas from the hymn *Ad coenam agni providi*,[3] beginning with stanza 6—*Consurgit Christus tumulo*—followed by stanza 7—*Quesumus, auctor omnium*—and stanza 8—*Gloria tibi, Domine*. A processional antiphon, *Cum rex glorie*—which recalls the Harrowing of Hell—concludes the *Elevatio*. At this point, the Matins service is resumed and continues to *Dum transisset*, whereupon the *Visitatio* opens. The most interesting feature of the *Visitatio* is the substitution of the sequence *Victime paschali laudes* instead of the closing *Surrexit Dominus*.[4]

The architecture of the church at Vadstena, which was designed by St. Birgitta herself and widely copied (e.g., at Maribo in Denmark), does not give many clues concerning how such ceremonies would have been presented.[5] The nuns occupied the upper gallery which covered the central portion of the nave, while the monks used their own choir at the back of the high altar where they could perhaps be seen by the nuns. The monks, however, could not see the nuns. The involvement of the nuns in the ceremonies at least as spectators should nevertheless be seen as almost a certainty.

---

[3]For the text of *Ad cenam agni prouidi*, see BrL II, Pt. 2, 387; see also the text in *Analecta Hymnica*, II, 46, as quoted by Young, *Drama of the Medieval Church*, I, 562. The manuscript reading *consurgit* is a variant of *cum surgit*. For the melody of the hymn, see Stäblein, ed., *Hymnen*, I, 189.

[4]For comparison, see Lipphardt, Nos. 100 (Châlons-sur-Marne[2]) and 143 (Paris[22]); see also Rankin, "The Music of the Medieval Liturgical Drama," p. 60.

[5]See Aron Andersson, *Vadstena Klosterkyrka*, Sveriges Kyrkor, 194 (Stockholm: Almqvist & Wiksell International, 1983), II, 11-18.

The manuscript is now housed in Riksarkivet in Stockholm where it has the shelf-mark Skoklostersamlingen, No. 2 (E 8899). Lipphardt's number is No. 447 (Link[2]).

<ELEVATIO CRUCIS et VISITATIO SEPULCHRI>

In sancta nocte d*omi*nice resur*reccio*nis ad eleuacione*m* crucis de sepulcro ca*n*tet*ur* hec a*ntiphona*

[*Antiphona.*] Surrexit d*omi*nus de sepulcro [Qui pro nobis pependit in ligno alleluia.[1]]

deinde isti *versus*

[*Hymnus.*] co*n*surgit[2] *christu*s tum*ul*o
[victor redit de baratro[3]
tirannum[4] trudens vinculo
et reserans paradisum].

q*ue*sum*us* auctor [omnium
in hoc paschali gaudio
ab omni mortis impetu
tuum defendas[5] populum].

glor*ia* tibi d*omi*ne
[qui surrexisti a mortuis
cum patre et sancto spiritu[6]
in sempiterna secula. Amen.[7]]

sequit*ur* a*ntiphona*

[*Antiphona.*] Cum rex glorie [*christu*s infernu*m* debellaturus in-

---

[1]Expansion of incipit of *Surrexit dominus* from BrL II, Pt. 2, 389; cf. AS III, 250, and LU 239 (CAO 5079).

[2]BrL, *Analecta Hymnica*: Cum surgit.

[3]*Analecta Hymnica*: barathro.

[4]*Analecta Hymnica*: tyrannum.

[5]*Analecta Hymnica*: defende.

[6]*Analecta Hymnica*: Patre et Sancto Spiritu.

[7]*Analecta Hymnica*: saecula. Expansion of incipit of *Ad cenam domini* from BrL II, Pt. 2, 387.

traret et chorus angelicus ante faciem eius portas princip*ium* tolli preciperet sanctor*um* populus qui tenebatur in morte captiuus voce lacrimabili clamauer*un*t aduenisti desiderabilis que*m* expectabamus in tenebris vt educeres hac nocte vinculatos de claustris te nostra vocabant suspiria te larga requirebant lamenta tu factus es spes desolatis magna consolacio in tormentis. Alleluya.[8]]

deinde ad matutt*inum*[9] *dicitur*

[*Antiphona*.] dom*i*ne labia [mea aperies et os meum adnuntiabit laudem tuam[10]].

[*Introit*.] deus in adiutor*ium* [meum intende
Domine ad adiuvandum me festina:
confundantur et revereantur
qui quaerunt animam meam.[11]
Gloria Patri, et Filio, et Spiritui Sancto. Sicut erat in principio, et nunc, et semper, et in saecula saeculorum. Amen.[12]]

Inuitator*ium*. Alleluya ter*tia*.

Ad noct*urnum* an*tiphona*. ego su*m* qui [sum et consilium meum non est cum impijs. sed in lege domini voluntas mea est alleluia.[13]]

p*salmus* [1.] bea*tus* vir [qui non abiit in consilio impiorum

---

[8]Incipit of *Cum rex glorie* expanded from No. 7 (Lipphardt 449a), below. This item appears in the earliest sources for the Sarum liturgy as a procession for Palm Sunday; see Terence Bailey, *The Processions of Sarum and the Western Church* (Toronto: Pontifical Institute of Mediaeval Studies, 1971), p. 166n.
[9]Helander: matutinas; Lipphardt: matutinam.
[10]Expansion of incipit of *Domine labia* from AM 352 (CAO 2355).
[11]Expansion of incipit of *Deus in adiutorium* from BSV (*Psalm* 69).
[12]LU 311.
[13]Expansion of incipit of *Ego sum* from BrL II, Pt. 2, 374 (CAO 2599); for music, see LC Q1ᵛ-Q2ʳ; cf. AS III, 235. The text is a paraphrase of portions of *Exodus* 3.14 and *Psalm* 1.1-2.

et in via peccatorum non stetit
et in cathedra pestilentiae non sedit
sed in lege Domini voluntas eius
et in lege eius meditabitur die ac nocte
et erit tanquam lignum
quod plantatum est secus decursus aquarum
quod fructum suum dabit in tempore suo
et folium eius non defluet
et omnia quaecumque faciet prosperabuntur
non sic impii non sic:
sed tamquam pulvis quem proicit ventus a facie terrae:
ideo non resurgent impii in iudicio
neque peccatores in concilio iustorum
quoniam novit Dominus viam iustorum
et iter impiorum peribit.[14]]

an*tiphona.* postulaui [patrem meum alleluia. dedit mihi gentes alleluia in hereditatem alleluia.[15]]

p*salmus* [2.] quare fre*muerunt* [gentes
et populi meditati sunt inania
adstiterunt reges terrae
et principes convenerunt in unum
adversus Dominum et adversus christum eius
disrumpamus vincula eorum
et proiciamus a nobis iugum ipsorum
qui habitat in caelis inridebit eos
et Dominus subsannabit eos
tunc loquetur ad eos in ira sua
et in furore suo conturbabit eos
ego autem constitutus sum rex ab eo
super Sion montem sanctum eius
praedicans praeceptum eius

---

[14]BSV.

[15]Expansion of incipit of *Postulaui* is from BrL II, Pt. 2, 374; for music see LC Q2^r. The text (CAO 4342) is a paraphrase of a portion of *Psalm* 2.8.

Dominus dixit ad me filius meus es tu
ego hodie genui te
postula a me et dabo tibi gentes hereditatem tuam
et possessionem tuam terminos terrae
reges eos in virga ferrea
tamquam vas figuli confringes eos
et nunc reges intellegite;
erudimini qui iudicatis terram
servite Domino in timore
et exultate ei in tremore
adprehendite disciplinam
nequando irascatur Dominus et pereatis de via iusta
cum exarserit in brevi ira eius
beati omnes qui confidunt in eo.[16]]

an*tiphona*. ego dormiui [et somnum cepi et exurrexi quia dominus
suscepit me alleluia alleluia.[17]]

p*salmu*s [3.] d*omi*ne quid [multiplicati sunt qui tribulant me
multi insurgunt adversum me
multi dicunt animae meae
non est salus ipsi in Deo eius:
tu autem Domine susceptor meus es
gloria mea et exaltans caput meum
voce mea ad Dominum clamavi
et exaudivit me de monte sancto suo
ego dormivi et soporatus sum
exsurrexi quia Dominus suscipiet me
non timebo milia populi circumdantis me
exsurge Domine salvum me fac Deus meus
quoniam tu percussisti omnes adversantes mihi sine causa
dentes peccatorum contrivisti

---

[16]BSV.

[17]Expansion of incipit of *Ego dormiui* from BrL II, Pt. 2, 374. For music, see LC Q2[v]; cf.
AS III, 235 (CAO 2572). The text is a paraphrase of *Psalm* 3.6.

Domini est salus et super populum tuum benedictio tua.[18]]

versus.[19] quem queris [mulier alleluia.
Responsorium. Uiuentem cum mortuis alleluia.[20]]

ew*angelium* marchi[21]

maria magdalen*a* [et maria iacobi et salome emerunt aromata: vt
venientes vngerent iesum. . . .[22]]

cum expo*sicione gregorii*[23]
[*Gregorij pape*. Audisti fratres charissimi quod sancte mulieres
que dominum secute fuerant cum aromatibus ad monumentum
venerunt: vt eum quem viuentem dilexerant etiam mortuo studio
humanitatis obsequuntur.[24]]

Responsorium. angel*us* do*mini* [descendit de celo et accedens
reuoluit lapidem et super eum sedit et dixit mulieribus nolite
timere scio enim quia crucifixum queritis. Jam surrexit venite et
videte locum vbi positus erat dominus alleluia[25]].

versus. angelus [domini locutus est mulieribus dicens quem queritis an iesum queritis. Jam *surrexit venite et videte locum vbi
positus erat dominus alleluia*[26]].

---

[18]BSV.

[19]This item should properly be designated as a *responsorium*.

[20]BrL II, Pt. 2, 374 (CAO 7468); for a musical setting, see WA III, 145.

[21]Helander: Marchi.

[22]Incipit of *Maria Magdalena* expanded from BrL II, Pt. 2, 375; for the completion of the
Gospel reading, see *Mark* 16.2-8.

[23]Helander: Gregorii.

[24]BrL II, Pt. 2, 375.

[25]Expansion of incipit of *Angelus Domini* from BrL II, Pt. 2, 375; for music, see LC
Q2^v-Q2^r; cf. AS III 235-36 (CAO 6093).

[26]Expansion of incipit of BrL II, Pt. 2, 375; for music, see LC Q3^r; cf. AS III, 236 (CAO
6093).

[*Lectio ij.* Sed res gesta aliud in sancta ecclesia significat gerendum. Sic quippe necesse est vt audiamus que facta sunt: quatinus cogitemus etiam que nobis sunt ex eorum imitatione facienda. Et nos igitur in eum qui mortuus est credentes: si odore virtutum refecti cum opinione bonorum operum dominum querimus: ad monumentum profecto illius cum aromatibus vennimus.[27]]

Responsorium. angelus do*mini* [locutus est cum mulieribus dicens quem queritis an iesum queritis. Jam surrexit venite et videte alleluia alleluia.[28]]

versus. (*blank*) [Ecce precedet vos in galyleam ibi eum videbitis sicut dixit vobis. Jam *surrexit venite et videte alleluia alleluia.*[29]]

[*Lectio iij.* Ille autem mulieres angelos vident que cum aromatibus venerunt: quia videlicet ille mentes supernos ciues aspiciunt que cum virtutum odoribus ad deum per sancta desideria proficiscuntur.[30]]

Responsorium. dum transisset [sabbatum maria magdalene et maria iacobi et salome emerunt aromata. Ut venientes vngerent iesum alleluia alleluia.[31]]

versus. et ualde mane [vna sabbatorum veniunt ad monumentum orto iam sole. *Ut venientes vngerent iesum alleluia alleluia.*[32]]

Responsorium repetit*ur.* [Dum transisset sabbatum maria magdalene et maria iacobi et salome emerunt aromata. Ut venientes vngerent iesum alleluia alleluia.] [Gloria patri et Filio, et Spiritui

---

[27]BrL II, Pt. 2, 375.

[28]BrL II, Pt. 2, 375; for music, see LC Q3^v-Q4^r; cf. AS III, 236 (CAO 6093).

[29]Versus from BrL II, Pt. 2, 375.

[30]BrL II, Pt. 2, 375.

[31]Expansion of incipit of *Dum transisset* from BrL II, Pt. 2, 375; for music, see LC Q4^v-R1^r; cf. AS III, 236-37 (CAO 6565).

[32]Expansion of incipit of *Et valde mane* is from BrL II, Pt. 2, 375; for music, see LC R1^r; cf. AS III, 237 (CAO 6565).

Sancto. Sicut erat in principio, et nunc, et semper, et in saecula saeculorum. Amen.[33]]

sic can*tantes p*rocedunt ad sepulcru*m*. *p*ercan*tato vero*[34] ulti*mo* R*esponsorio* ecce tres *c*lerici pro *m*ulierib*us* in capis veniu*n*t ad sepulcru*m* cu*m* thurib*u*lo *et* incenso. sed*entibus* intro duob*us* dya*ch*onib*us* in dalmaticis pro angelis. sicq*ue* submissa voce qui extra stan*t* ǀ incipie*n*t an*tiphonam*

quis reuoluet [nobis lapide*m* ab hostio monumenti al*leluia* al-leluia.[35]]

*res*po*n*de*n*t clara voce deintus sede*n*tes an*tiphona*

que*m* queritis [in sepulchro o *ch*risticole.[36]]

Item extra stan*tes*

ih*esu*m nazarenu*m*

*res*po*n*dent dein*tus*

non est hic [sed surrexit]

et addu*n*t

venite et videte [locum, ubi positus erat Dominus, Alleluia.[37]]

tu*n*c intre*n*t *et* thurifice*n*t locu*m*.

addu*n*tque angeli

---

[33]LU 311.

[34]Schmid: uno.

[35]Incipit expanded from No. 2 (Lipphardt 448), above.

[36]Incipit expanded from No. 2 (Lipphardt 448), above.

[37]LC Q3ʳ-Q3ᵛ; cf. AS III, 236 (CAO 5352).

cito eu*n*tes [dicite discipulis eius et petro quia surrexit dominus alleluia.[38]]

et tollant m*u*lieres linteami*n*a proceda*n*tq*u*e ad p*op*ul*u*m clara voce ca*n*tan*t*es

victime paschali laudes [immolant christiani.
Agnus redemit oues christus innocens patri reconciliauit peccatores.
Mors et vita duello conflixere mirando dux vite mortuus regnat viuus.
Dic nobis maria quid vidisti in via:
sepulcrum christi viuentis et gloriam vidi resurgentis.
Angelicos testes sudarium et vestes
surrexit christus spes nostra precedet suos in galyleam.
Credendum est magis soli marie veraci
quam iudeorum turbe fallaci.[39]
Scimus christum surrexisse a mortuis vere
tu nobis victor rex miserere alleluia.[40]]

Hiis finitis incipit cantor

Te d*eu*m [laudamus: te Dominum confitemur.
Te aeternum Patrem omnis terra veneratur.
Tibi omnes Angeli, tibi Caeli et universae Potestates:
Tibi Cherubim et Seraphim incessabili voce proclamant:
Sanctus: Sanctus: Sanctus Dominus Deus Sabaoth.
Pleni sunt caeli et terra majestatis gloriae tuae.
Te gloriosus Apostolorum chorus:
Te Prophetarum laudabilis numerus:
Te Martyrum candidatus laudat exercitus.
Te per orbem terrarum sancta confitetur Ecclesia:

---

[38]Expansion of incipit of *Cito euntes* from BrL II, Pt. 2, 390; see also AS III, 250 (CAO 1813).

[39]This unpleasantly anti-semitic stanza is omitted in LU 780.

[40]Expansion of incipit of *Victime Pascali* from BrL II, Pt. 2, 375-76.

Patrem immensae majestatis:
Venerandum tuum verum, et unicum Filium:
Sanctum quoque Paraclitum Spiritum.
Tu Rex gloriae, Christe.
Tu Patris sempiternus es Filius.
Tu ad liberandum suscepturus hominem,
non horruisti Virginis uterum.
Tu devicto mortis aculeo, aperuisti credentibus regna caelorum.
Tu ad dexteram Dei sedes, in gloria Patris.
Judex crederis esse venturus.
Te ergo quaesumus, tuis famulis subveni, quos pretioso sanguine redemisti.
Aeterna fac cum Sanctis tuis in gloria numerari.
Salvum fac populum tuum Domine, et benedic hereditati tuae.
Et rege eos, et extolle illos usque in aeternum.
Per singulos dies, benedicimus te.
Et laudamus nomen tuum in saeculorum, et in saeculum saeculi.
Dignare Domine die isto sine peccato nos custodire.
Miserere nostri Domine, miserere nostri.
Fiat misericordia tua Domine super nos, quemadmodum speravimus in te.
In te Domine speravi: non confundar in aeternum.[41]]

compulsatis interim *omnibus* signis. postea no*n dicitur versus nec deus* in adiutor*ium.* s*ed* statim im*poni*tu*r an*ti*phona* ad laudes et sic reu*ertun*tu*r* ad chor*um.*

<THE ELEVATION OF THE CROSS and THE VISIT TO THE SEPULCHER>

In the holy night of Resurrection Sunday at the elevation of the cross from the sepulcher, this antiphon is sung:

---

[41]LU 1832-34.

The Lord, who for our sake hung upon the tree, is risen from the grave. Alleluia, alleluia, alleluia.

Then these verses [follow]:

When Christ arose from the grave,
returning as a victor from hell,
he forcibly chained the tyrant
and opened paradise again.

Creator of all, we pray you,
in this Easter joy,
protect your people
from all the onslaughts of death.

Glory to you, Lord,
who have risen from the dead,
With the Father and Holy Spirit,
world without end. Amen.

The antiphon follows:

When Christ the king of glory, to vanquish hell, entered and overturned the gates of hell's kingdom, with the angel choir before him, those holy ones who were held captive in death cried out with tearful voice, "You have come, desired of nations, for whom we in chains have waited in darkness to lead us this night from prison. Our sighs cried out, great laments reached up to you. You have become the hope of the desolate, the great consolation of those in torment. Alleluia."

From that point at Matins it is said:

Antiphon. Lord, open my lips, and my mouth shall show forth your praise.

Introit. O God, make speed to save me: O Lord, make haste to help me. Let them be confounded and put to shame who seek after my soul. Glory to the Father and to the Son and to the Holy Spirit. As it was in the beginning, is now, and ever shall be, world without end. Amen.

Invitatory. Alleluia, alleluia, alleluia.

At nocturn, the antiphon. I am who am, and my counsel is not with the ungodly: but my delight is in the law of the Lord, alleluia.

Psalm 1. Blessed is the man who has not walked in the counsel of the ungodly,
nor stood in the way of sinners, nor sat in the chair of pestilence.
But his will is in the law of the Lord,
and on his law he shall meditate day and night.
And he shall be like a tree which is planted near the running waters,
which shall bring forth its fruit, in due season.
And his leaf shall not fall off:
and all whatsoever he shall do shall prosper.
Not so the wicked, not so:
but they are like the dust, which the wind drives from the face of the earth.
Therefore the wicked shall not rise again in judgment:
nor sinners in the council of the just.
For the Lord knows the way of the just:
and the way of the wicked shall perish.

Antiphon. I have asked my father, alleluia, and he has given me the nations as my heritage, alleluia.

Psalm 2. Why have the Gentiles raged,
and the people devised vain things?
The kings of the earth stood up, and the princes met together,
against the Lord, and against his Christ.
Let us break their bonds asunder:

and let us cast away their yoke from us.
He that dwells in heaven shall laugh at them:
and the Lord shall deride them.
Then shall he speak to them in his anger,
and trouble them in his rage.
But I am appointed king by him over Sion his holy mountain,
preaching his commandment.
The Lord has said to me: You are my son,
this day have I begotten you.
Ask of me, and I will give you the Gentiles for your inheritance,
And the utmost parts of the earth for your possession.
You shall rule them with a rod of iron,
and shall break them in pieces like a potter's vessel.
And now, O you kings, understand;
receive instruction, you that judge the earth.
Serve you the Lord with fear:
and rejoice unto him with trembling.
Embrace discipline, lest at any time the Lord be angry,
and you perish from the just way.
When his wrath shall be kindled in a short time,
blessed are all they that trust in him.

Antiphon. I have slept and have taken my rest, and I have risen up again because the Lord sustained me, alleluia, alleluia.

Psalm 3. Why, O Lord, are they multiplied that afflict me?
many are they who rise up against me.
Many say to my soul:
There is no salvation for him in his God.
But you, O Lord, are my protector,
my glory, and the lifter up of my head.
I have cried to the Lord with my voice:
and he has heard me from his holy hill.
I have slept and have taken my rest:
and I have risen up, because the Lord has protected me.
I will not fear thousands of the people, surrounding me:
arise, O Lord; save me, O my God.

For you have struck all them who are my adversaries without cause:
you have broken the teeth of sinners.
Salvation is of the Lord:
and your blessing is upon your people.

Verse. Whom do you seek, woman? Alleluia.
Responsory. I seek the living among the dead.

The Gospel according to Mark.

[In that time.] *Antiphon.* Mary Magdalene and Mary Jacobi and Salome bought spices, seeking to anoint the Lord. . . .

With commentary by Gregory.
Pope Gregory. [Lesson I]. You have heard, dearly beloved brothers, how the holy women who had followed the Lord came with spices to the tomb, and how, since they loved him when he was alive, they planned to honor him, now that he had died, with proofs of their love.

Responsory. The angel of the Lord came down from heaven, and as he came closer, he rolled away the stone and sat upon it. And he said to the women, "Fear not. I know that you seek the crucified one. He is risen. Come and see the place where the Lord was laid, alleluia."

Verse. The angel of the Lord spoke to the women and said, "Whom do you seek? Is it not Jesus you seek? He is risen. Come and see the place where the Lord was laid, alleluia."

Lesson II. But this that they did signifies what the members of the holy Church should be doing. We must listen to what was done so that we may learn what to do to imitate those things. And we who believe in him who has died, if we are characterized by the good odor of virtue and by a reputation for good works, may be said to come to the sepulcher with sweet spices.

Responsory. The angel of the Lord spoke to the women and said, "Whom do you seek? Is it not Jesus you seek? He is risen. Come and see, alleluia, alleluia."

Verse. (blank) [Behold, he goes before you into Galilee where you will see him, as he said. He is risen. Come and see, alleluia, alleluia.]

Lesson III. However, the women who had brought spices saw the angels; thus souls, fragrant in their virtue, come to the vision of the celestial citizens as they are drawn toward the Lord by their holy desires. . . .

Responsory. When the sabbath had ended, Mary Magdalene and Mary the mother of James and Salome bought spices and came to anoint Jesus, alleluia, alleluia.

Verse. And indeed, early one sabbath morning they came to the grave as at the rising of the sun. Thus they came to anoint Jesus, alleluia, alleluia.

Responsory, repeated. When the sabbath had ended, Mary Magdalene and Mary, the mother of James, and Salome bought spices. Thus they came to anoint Jesus, alleluia, alleluia. Glory to the Father and to the Son and to the Holy Spirit. As it was in the beginning, is now, and ever shall be, world without end. Amen.

So singing, they proceed to the sepulcher. After singing the responsory for the last time, the three clerics representing women in copes come to the sepulcher with thurible and incense. Seated inside are two deacons in dalmatics as angels. In a low, soft voice those who stand outside begin the antiphon:

"Who will roll the stone away from the door of the tomb for us? Alleluia, alleluia."

Then those seated respond in a clear, strong voice:

"Whom do you seek in the sepulcher, O Christians?"

Those standing outside say:

"Jesus of Nazareth."

Then they respond from inside:

"He is not here, but he is risen."

And they add:

"Come and see the place where the Lord was laid, alleluia."

Then they should enter and cense the place.

The angels add:

"Go quickly and tell the disciples and Peter that the Lord is risen, alleluia."

The women should pick up the linens and proceed to the people singing in a clear, strong voice:

To the paschal victim
Christians may offer praise.
The sheep are ransomed by the Lamb;
and the innocent Christ
has reconciled sinners to his Father.

The miraculous conflict of death and life
is ended;
the champion of life, though slain,
lives to reign.

Tell us, Mary,
what did you see on the way?
The tomb which the living enclosed;
I saw Christ's glory as he rose.
The angels there testified
as did the shroud with grave-clothes.
Christ, my hope, is risen:
He will go before you into Galilee.

The truthful Mary is more to be believed
than the untruthful crowd of Jews.[42]
We know that Christ is truly risen
from the dead:
Show us your mercy, victorious king.]

When they have finished, the cantor begins:

We praise you, God: we acknowledge you to be the Lord.
You are the eternal Father: the whole world worships you.
To you all the angels, the heavens, and all the Powers, Cherubim and Seraphim, proclaim aloud unceasingly,
"Holy, holy, holy Lord, God of Sabaoth.
Heaven and earth are full of the majesty of your glory."
The glorious company of the apostles, the laudable host of prophets, the white-clad band of martyrs praise you.
The holy Church throughout the whole earth confesses that you are the Father of unlimited majesty; true and worthy of honor, your only Son; also the holy Spirit, the comforter.
You are the king of glory, O Christ. You are the eternal Son of the Father.
When you came to liberate humans, you did not scorn the Virgin's womb.
You overcame the sting of Death: you opened the kingdom of heaven to all believers.
You are seated at the right hand of God, in the glory of the Father:

---

[42]See note 39, above.

we believe that you will come to be our judge.
We therefore ask that you come and help your people, whom you
have redeemed with your precious blood.
Cause them to be counted with your saints in eternal glory.
Save your people, Lord, and bless your inheritance.
Rule them, and raise them up in eternity.
Daily we bless you and we praise your name, world without end.
Keep us, Lord, this day without sin.
Have mercy on us, Lord, have mercy on us.
Let your mercy, Lord, be upon us, as we have trusted in you.
In you, Lord, have I trusted. I will never be confounded.

*At the tolling of all the bells, afterwards the verse "O God, make
speed" is not said. But the antiphon for Lauds occurs immediately,
and thus they return to the choir.*

5

Visitatio Sepulchri
from a Swedish Breviary

A unique Type II *Visitatio sepulchri* (one containing the
race of the disciples Peter and John to the sepulcher) is found
in a manuscript fragment from a Breviary of the thirteenth
or fourteenth century from the use of an unknown Swedish
church.[1] Possessing red rubrics, black lettering and medium-
sized black initials, and three larger red and blue initials,[2]
the text is fully noted, with two styles of musical notation—
one style using regular square notes and another in a sim-
pler, sketchier style. These two styles indicate that the first
music scribe, who also may have been the text scribe, began
writing in the musical notation, adapting melodies usually
associated with Type I texts; however, he only completed the
items *Quis reuoluit*, *Quem queritis*, *Ihesum nazarenum*, *Non
est hic*, and *Uenite et uidete* as well as *Currebant duo simul*
and *Surrexit Dominus*. The second music scribe, who was
much less skilled, filled in the missing items: *Maria magdalena*, *Ad monumentum*, and *Cernitis o socii*. This scribe provided melodies that have been associated with Type II texts

---

[1]Schmid, pp. 2, 5; Lipphardt, VI, 432.
[2]The larger initials are M (Maria), A (Angelus), and D (Deus).

rather than with Type I texts.[3]

The present play is based on a German model,[4] possibly the Type II *Visitatio* from Halberstadt (Lipphardt, Nos. 578, 582, 584). The Halberstadt example introduces the response of the angel in a distinctive form—*Quem queritis, o tremule mulieres, in hoc tumulo plorantes*—which is also preserved in this Swedish *Visitatio*. However, because the musical setting of this item is not drawn from a similar model, it differs substantially from the Halberstadt *Visitatio*:[5]

Except for the *Currebant*, the music of the Swedish Type II *Visitatio* is in fact unrelated to that of Halberstadt so long as the musical notation is the work of the main scribe; the items copied in by the second (and much less skilled) scribe—*Maria Magdalena*, *Ad monumentum*, and *Cernitis*—are, however, melodically similar and are characteristically German.[6]

---

[3]My comments on the relationship of the Type II text to its musical settings are indebted to Michael Norton.

[4]Lipphardt, VI, 432.

[5]Musical transcription in Michael Norton, "Of Stages and Types in *Visitatione Sepulchri*," pp. 142-44.

[6]Rankin, "The Music of the Medieval Liturgical Drama," pp. 114, 127, 136.

The fragment consists of two leaves, measuring 40 x 27 cm. unfolded and 34.5 x 23.5 cm. folded, and is dry parchment with a number of creases. The fragment, listed under the shelfmark *Räkenskaper för Varuhus o. Handling* at Riksarkivet in Stockholm, is attached as covers to provincial records from Älfsborg/Lödöse of 1576-1581. Lipphardt, who identifies it as Vitterhetsakademien Br. 285, lists it as No. 451 (Stock[2]).

<VISITATIO SEPULCHRI>

. . . pro angelis. sic*que* submissa uoce qui extra[1] stant incipiunt antiphonam.

Maria magdalena et alia maria ferebant diluculo aromata dominum querentes in monumento.

Extra stantes incipiant ha*nc* a*ntiphonam*.

Quis reuoluit nobis ab hostio[2] lapide*m* <quem> regere[3] *s*a*nctu*m cernimus sepulchr*u*m.

Responde*a*nt deintus sedentes. ant*iphonam*.

Quem queritis o tremule mulieres in hoc tumulo plorantes.

Extra stantes a*ntiphonam*.

Ihesum nazarenum crucifixum querimus.

Ang*eli*s hanc ant*iphonam*.

Non est hic ⌈que*m*⌉ queritis sed scito[4] euntes nunciate discipulis eius et petro quia surrexit ihesus.

a*ntiphona*. Uenite *et* uidete locum ubi posit*us* erat d*omi*nus al*lel*via a*llel*via.

Mulieres istam antipho*n*am.

---

[1]Lipphardt: intra. Schmid omits the entire rubric.
[2]Lipphardt: ostio.
[3]Lipphardt: tegere; this emendation is correct, since *regere* is clearly a scribal error for *tegere*.
[4]Lipphardt: cito (emendation of scribal error).

Ad monumentum uenimus gementes angelum domini sedentem uidimus et dicentem quia surrexit ihesus.

antiphona. Currebant duo simul et ille alius discipulus precucurrit cicius petro et uenit prior ad monumentum allelvia.[5]

antiphona. Cernitis o socii ecce lintheamina et sudarium | et corpus non est inuentum.

antiphona. Surrexit dominus de sepulchro qui pro nobis pependit in ligno alleluya.

finita antiphona incipit cantor

Te Deum laudamus [te Dominum confitemur.
Te aeternum Patrem omnis terra veneratur.
Tibi omnes Angeli, tibi Caeli et universae Potestates:
Tibi Cherubim et Seraphim incessabili voce proclamant:
Sanctus: Sanctus: Sanctus Dominus Deus Sabaoth.
Pleni sunt caeli et terra majestatis gloriae tuae.
Te gloriosus Apostolorum chorus:
Te Prophetarum laudabilis numerus:
Te Martyrum candidatus laudat exercitus.
Te per orbem terrarum sancta confitetur Ecclesia:
Patrem immensae majestatis:
Venerandum tuum verum, et unicum Filium:
Sanctum quoque Paraclitum Spiritum.
Tu Rex gloriae, Christe.
Tu Patris sempiternus es Filius.
Tu ad liberandum suscepturus hominem,
non horruisti Virginis uterum.
Tu devicto mortis aculeo, aperuisti credentibus regna caelorum.
Tu ad dexteram Dei sedes, in gloria Patris.
Judex crederis esse venturus.
Te ergo quaesumus, tuis famulis subveni, quos pretioso sanguine

---

[5]Cf. AM 465.

redemisti.
Aeterna fac cum Sanctis tuis in gloria numerari.
Salvum fac populum tuum Domine, et benedic hereditati tuae.
Et rege eos, et extolle illos usque in aeternum.
Per singulos dies, benedicimus te.
Et laudamus nomen tuum in saeculorum, et in saeculum saeculi.
Dignare Domine die isto sine peccato nos custodire.
Miserere nostri Domine, miserere nostri.
Fiat misericordia tua Domine super nos, quemadmodum speravimus in te.
In te Domine speravi: non confundar in aeternum.[6]]

Compulsantibus interim omnibus signis. postea non dicitur versus nec. Deus in adiutorium. Sed statim imponitur antiphona ad laudes.

antiphona. Angelus autem domini descendit de celo et accedens reuoluit lapidem et sedebat super eum alleluya allelvia. [Gloria Patri, et Filio, et Spiritui Sancto. Sicut erat in principio, et nunc, et semper, et in saecula[7]] seculorum amen.

THE VISIT TO THE SEPULCHER

. . . taking the angels' role. Those standing outside intone the antiphon in a low, soft voice:

Mary Magdalene and the other Mary early in the morning brought spices, seeking the Lord in the tomb.

Those standing outside intone this antiphon:

"Who will roll away from the door for us the stone which we saw

---

[6]LU 1832-34.
[7]*Gloria Patri* expanded from LU 311.

covering the holy tomb?"

Those seated inside should reply with this antiphon:

"Whom do you seek, O quaking women, weeping at this tomb?"

Those outside [sing] the antiphon:

"We seek Jesus of Nazareth, crucified."

The angels [sing] this antiphon:

"He whom you seek is not here, but go quickly and tell his disciples and Peter that Jesus has risen."

Antiphon. Come and see the place where the Lord was laid, alleluia, alleluia.

The women sing the antiphon:

"Mourning we came to the grave site, and we saw an angel of the Lord sitting there, telling us that Jesus has risen."

Antiphon. The two ran together, and the other disciple arrived more quickly than Peter and went before him into the tomb, alleluia.

Antiphon. Behold, O companions, the winding sheet and the napkin, but the body is not found.

Antiphon. The Lord, who for our sake hung upon the tree, is risen from the grave.

At the end of the antiphon, the cantor begins:

We praise you, God: we acknowledge you to be the Lord.
You are the eternal Father: the whole world worships you.

To you all the angels, the heavens, and all the Powers, Cherubim and Seraphim, proclaim aloud unceasingly,
"Holy, holy, holy Lord, God of Sabaoth.
Heaven and earth are full of the majesty of your glory."
The glorious company of the apostles, the laudable host of prophets, the white-clad band of martyrs praise you.
The holy Church throughout the whole earth confesses that you are the Father of unlimited majesty; true and worthy of honor, your only Son; also the holy Spirit, the comforter.
You are the king of glory, O Christ. You are the eternal Son of the Father.
When you came to liberate humans, you did not scorn the Virgin's womb.
You overcame the sting of Death; you opened the kingdom of heaven to all believers.
You are seated at the right hand of God, in the glory of the Father: we believe that you will come to be our judge.
We therefore ask that you come and help your people, whom you have redeemed with your precious blood.
Cause them to be counted with your saints in eternal glory.
Save your people, Lord, and bless your inheritance.
Rule them, and raise them up in eternity.
Daily we bless you and we praise your name, world without end.
Keep us, Lord, this day without sin.
Have mercy on us, Lord, have mercy on us.
Let your mercy, Lord, be upon us, as we have trusted in you.
In you, O Lord, have I trusted. I will never be confounded.

At the tolling of all the bells, afterwards the verse "O God, make speed" is not said. But the antiphon for Lauds is begun immediately.

[*Antiphon.*] The angel of the Lord came down from heaven, and rolled away the stone and sat upon it, alleluia, alleluia. Glory to the Father, and to the Son, and to the Holy Spirit. As it was in the beginning, is now, and will be forever, world without end. Amen.

6

Elevatio Crucis and *Visitatio Sepulchri* from a Linköping Ordinal (1493)

An Ordinal of 1493 in the use of the Linköping diocese and identified with Linköping Cathedral contains an *Elevatio crucis* and a *Visitatio sepulchri*, the latter a Type I drama and thus lacking the race of Peter and John. The text is written on paper in a cursive hand. The book itself is a small leather-bound volume measuring 21.1 x 14 cm., and is held by the Uppsala University Library under the shelfmark C. 428. As is typical in the case of an Ordinal, it lacks notation. Folio 37 contains the pertinent ceremonies.

The *Elevatio* is indicated to be done prior to Easter Matins and is attached directly to the *Visitatio*. In the *Visitatio*, the *Victime paschali laudes* once again replaces the more common *Surrexit Dominus* immediately before the *Te Deum*.

While there is a fine sculpture (fig. 2) from a portal at Linköping Cathedral (removed earlier in this century and not *in situ*) illustrating the angel and the holy women at a coffer tomb (the grave clothes are draped over the edge of the tomb, and the soldiers are to be seen below), there is now no evidence of an Easter sepulcher present in the building. The final rubric, which has also appeared in the manuscript associated with Vadstena, seems to suggest presentation of the *Visitatio* outside the choir of the cathedral since the clergy are directed to return to that location. If German rather than English influence on the location of the sepulcher is to be conjectured, the structure might have been placed in the nave instead of at the north side of the chancel near the high altar. And it is even possible that the sepulcher at Linköping Cathedral might have been similar to that depicted in the sculpture from the portal.

Lipphardt's number for these ceremonies is No. 449 (Link[4]).

\<ELEVATIO CRUCIS et VISITATIO SEPULCHRI\>

In Sancta Nocte Dominice resurrectionis ad eleuationem crucis cantetur hec antiphona

(scratched out)

Surrexit dominus [de sepulcro qui pro nobis pependit in ligno alleluia.[1]]

Cum versibus[2]

Cum surgit [christus tumulo
victor redit de baratro[3]
tirannum[4] trudens vinculo
et reserans paradisum.]

Quesumus auctor [omnium
in hoc paschali gaudio
ab omni mortis impetu
tuum defendas[5] populum.]

Gloria tibi domine
[qui surrexisti a mortuis
cum patre et sancto spiritu[6]
in sempiterna secula.[7] Amen.[8]]

---

[1]Expansion of incipit of *Surrexit Dominus* from BrL II, Pt. 2, 389; see also AS III, 250; cf. LU 239 (CAO 7739).

[2]Lipphardt: Versu.

[3]*Analecta Hymnica*: barathro.

[4]*Analecta Hymnica*: tyrannum.

[5]*Analecta Hymnica*: defende.

[6]*Analecta Hymnica*: Patre et Sancto Spiritu.

[7]*Analecta Hymnica*: saecula.

[8]Expansion of the stanzas of *Ad coenum agni prouidi* from BrL II, Pt. 2, 387. For music, see Stäblein, I, 189.

sequit*ur*

Cum rex glorie [*ch*ristus infernu*m* debellaturus intraret et chorus angelicus ante faciem eius portas principi*um* tolli preciperet sanctoru*m* populus qui tenebatur in morte captiuus voce lacrimabili clamaueru*nt* aduenisti desiderabilis que*m* expectabamus in tenebris vt educeres hac nocte vinculatos de claustris te nostra vocabant suspiria te larga requirebant lamenta tu factus es spes desolatis magna consolacio in tormentis. Alleluya.[9]]

deinde ad matut*inas dicitur*

[*Antiphona.*] Dom*in*e labia [mea aperies et os meum adnuntiabit laudem tuam.[10]]

[*Introitus.*] De*us* in adiuto*rium* [meum intende
Domine ad adiuvandum me festina:
confundantur et revereantur
qui quaerunt animam meam.[11]
Gloria Patri, et Filio, et Spiritui Sancto. Sicut erat in principio, et nunc, et semper, et in saecula saeculorum. Amen.[12]]

Inuitat*orium.* al*l*elu*i*a al*l*elu*i*a al*l*elu*i*a

Ad noc*turno* an*tiphona*

Ego sum [qui sum et consilium meum non est cum impijs. sed in lege domini voluntas mea est alleluia[13]].

ps*almus* [1.] Bea*tus* vir [qui non abiit in consilio impiorum

---

[9]Incipit expanded from No. 7 (Lipphardt 449a), below.

[10]Expansion of incipit of *Domine labia* from BSV (*Psalm* 50.17); for music, see AM 352.

[11]Expansion of incipit of *Psalm* 69.1-3 from BSV.

[12]LU 1027-28; for *Gloria Patri*, see LU 311.

[13]Expansion of incipit of *Ego sum* is from BrL II, Pt. 2, 374. For music, see LC Q1ᵛ-Q2ʳ; cf. AS III, 235 (CAO 2599). The text is a paraphrase of portions of *Exodus* 3.14 and *Psalm* 1.1-2.

et in via peccatorum non stetit
et in cathedra pestilentiae non sedit
sed in lege Domini voluntas eius
et in lege eius meditabitur die ac nocte
et erit tamquam lignum
quod plantatum est secus decursus aquarum
quod fructum suum dabit in tempore suo
et folium eius non defluet
et omnia quaecumque faciet prosperabuntur
non sic impii non sic:
Sed tamquam pulvis quem proicit ventus a facie terrae:
ideo non resurgent impii in iudicio
neque peccatores in concilio iustorum
quoniam novit Dominus viam iustorum
et iter impiorum peribit.[14]]

antiphona. Postulaui [patrem meum alleluia. dedit mihi gentes alleluia in hereditatem alleluia.[15]]

ps*almus* [2.] Quare fre*muerunt* [gentes
et populi meditati sunt inania
adstiterunt reges terrae
et principes convenerunt in unum
adversus Dominum et adversus christum eius
disrumpamus vincula eorum
et proiciamus a nobis iugum ipsorum
qui habitat in caelis inridebit eos
et Dominus subsannabit eos
tunc loquetur ad eos in ira sua
et in furore suo conturbabit eos
ego autem constitutus sum rex ab eo
super Sion montem sanctum eius
praedicans praeceptum eius

---

[14]Expansion of incipit of *Psalm* 1 from BSV.
[15]Expansion of incipit of *Postulaui patrem meam* from BrL II, Pt. 2, 374. See also LC Q2ʳ.
The text is a paraphrase of a portion of *Psalm* 2.8.

Dominus dixit ad me filius meus es tu
ego hodie genui te
postula a me et dabo tibi gentes hereditatem tuam
et possessionem tuam terminos terrae
reges eos in virga ferrea
tamquam vas figuli confringes eos
et nunc reges intelligite;
erudimini qui iudicatis terram
servite Domino in timore
et exultate ei cum tremore
adprehendite disciplinam
nequando irascatur Dominus et pereatis de via iusta
cum exarserit in brevi ira eius
beata omnes qui confidunt in eo.[16]]

antiphona. Ego dormiui [et somnum cepi et exurrexi quia dominus suscepit me alleluia alleluia.[17]]

ps*almus* [3.] <Domi>ni quid m*ulti*p*licati* [sunt qui tribulant me
multi insurgunt adversum me
multi dicunt animae meae
non est salus ipsi in Deo eius:
tu autem Domine susceptor meus es
gloria mea et exaltans caput meum
voce mea ad Dominum clamavi
et exaudivit me de monte sancto suo
ego dormivi et soporatus sum
exsurrexi quia Dominus suscipiet me
non timebo milia populi circumdantis me
exsurge Domine salvum me fac Deus meus
quoniam tu percussisti omnes adversantes mihi sine causa
dentes peccatorum contrivisti

---

[16]Expansion of incipit of *Psalm* 2 is from BSV.

[17]Expansion of incipit of *Ego dormiui* is from BrL II, Pt. 2, 374; for music, see LC Q2[v], and also AS III, 235 (CAO 2572). The text is a paraphrase of *Psalm* 3.6.

Domini est salus et super populum tuum benedictio tua[18]].

versus. Que*m* que*ris* muli*er* [alleluia.
R*esponsorium.* Uiuentum cum mortuis alleluia.[19]]

ewa*ngelium* Marci[20]

[In illo tempore.] Maria magda*lena* [et maria iacobi et salome
emerunt aromata: vt venientes vngerent iesum. . . .[21]]

cum exposit*ione gregorii*[22]
[*Gregorij pape.* Audistis fratres charissimi quod sancte muliers
que dominum secute fuerant cum aromatibus ad monumentum
venerunt: vt eum quem viuentem dilexerant etiam mortuo studio
humanitatis obsequuntur.[23]]

R*esponsorium.* Angelu*s* Dom*ini* [descendit de celo et accedens
reuoluit lapidem et super eum sedit et dixit mulieribus nolite
timere scio enim quia crucifixum queritis. Jam surrexit venite et
videte locum vbi positus erat dominus alleluia.[24]]

versus. angelu*s* [domini locutus est mulieribus dicens quem queritis an iesum queritis. Jam *surrexit venite et videte locum vbi
positus erat dominus alleluia.*[25]]

---

[18]Expansion of incipit of *Psalm* 3 is from BSV.

[19]BrL II, Pt. 2, 374. See also CAO 7468; for a musical setting, see WA 145.

[20]See Helander, p. 335.

[21]Incipit of *Maria magdalena* expanded from BrL II, Pt. 2, 375; for the completion of the
Gospel reading, see *Mark* 16.2-8.

[22]See Helander, p. 335.

[23]BrL II, Pt. 2, 375.

[24]Expansion of incipit of *Angelus Domini descendit* from BrL II, Pt. 2, 375; for music, see
LC Q2ᵛ-Q3ᵛ; cf. AS III, 235-36, and CAO 6093.

[25]Expansion of versus *Angelus Domini locutus est* from BrL II, Pt. 2, 375; for music, see
LC Q3ᵛ; cf. AS III, 236 (CAO 6093).

[*Lectio ij.* Sed res gesta aliud in sancta ecclesia significat gerendum. Sic quippe necesse est vt audiamus que facta sunt: quatinus cogitemus etiam que nobis sunt ex eorum imitatione facienda. Et nos igitur in eum qui mortuus est credentes: si odore virtutum refecti cum opinione bonorum operum dominum querimus: ad monumentum profecto illius cum aromatibus venimus.[26]]

Responsorium. Angelus Domini locutus [est cum mulieribus dicens quem queritis an iesum queritis. Jam surrexit venite et videte alleluia alleluia.
Versus. Ecce precedet vos in galyleam ibi eum videbitis sicut dixit vobis. Jam *surrexit venite et videte alleluia alleluia.*[27]]

[*Lectio III.* Ille autem mulieres angelos vident que cum aromatibus venerunt: quia videlicet ille mentes supernos ciues aspiciunt que cum virtutum odoribus ad deum per sancta desideria proficiscuntur. . . .[28]]

~~Responsorium.~~ Dum *transisset* [sabbatum maria magdalene et maria iacobi et salome emerunt aromata. Ut venientes vngerent iesum alleluia alleluia.[29]]

Versus. Et valde [mane vna sabbatorum veniunt ad monumentum orto iam sole. Ut *venientes vngerent iesum alleluia alleluia.*[30]]
Gloria Patri [et Filio, et Spiritui Sancto. Sicut erat in principio, et nunc, et semper, et in saecula saeculorum. Amen.[31]]

---

[26]BrL II, Pt. 2, 375.

[27]Expansion of incipits of responsorium *Angelus Domini locutus est* and versus *Ecce precedet vos* from BrL II, Pt. 2, 375; for music, see LC Q3^v-Q4^r; cf. AS III, 236 (CAO 6093).

[28]BrL II, Pt. 2, 375.

[29]Expansion of incipit of *Dum transisset* from BrL II, Pt. 2, 375; for music, see LC Q4^v-R1^r; cf. AS III, 236-37 (CAO 6565).

[30]Expansion of incipit of *Et valde mane* from BrL II, Pt. 2, 375; for music, see LC R1^r; cf. AS III, 237 (CAO 6565).

[31]LU 311. The incipit *Gloria Patri* is written in the margin of the page.

Repetit*ur* R*esponsorium*. [D*um* *transisset* sabbatum maria magdalene et maria iacobi et salome emerunt aromata. Ut venientes
vngerent iesum alleluia alleluia.]

solet tamen fieri hac nocte post responsorium illud Dum transisset
etc. quedam solempnior representacio resurrectionis ihesu christi
quam si imitar volueris eius modum require.[32]

Sic *cantantes* *procedunt* ad *sepulchr*um et *percantato*[33] vltimo
R*esponsorium* ecce tres *clerici* *pro* *mulieribus* *in* capis *veniunt* ad
*sepulchr*um *cum* *turribulis* *et* incenso *sedentibus* *intro* duob*us*
dyaconibus *in* dalmatic*is* *pro* angelis *sicque* submissa voce qui
extra stant incipiant ant*iphona*

Quis reuoluet nobis [lapid*em* ab hostio monumenti a*lleluia* alleluia.[34]]

R*espo*nd*ent* clara voce qui int*us* sede*ntes* a*ntiphona*

Que*m* querit*is* | [in sepulchro]

Ex*tra* stant*es*

Ih*esum* nazare*num*

Int*us* r*espo*nd*ent*

Non e*st* hic [sed surrexit]

et addu*nt*

---

[32]Marginal notation at top of fol. Hii. This marginal note is very hard to read, and I am
depending in part on Schmid's transcription (p. 5n). It is not printed by Lipphardt.
[33]Schmid: *omit* et percantato.
[34]Expansion of incipit of *Quis reuoluet* from No. 2 (Lipphardt 448), above.

Venite et vid*e*te [locum, ubi positus erat Dominus, Alleluia.[35]]

tun*c* intren*t et* thurificen*t* locu*m*

Addun*tqu*e angeli

Cito euntes [dicite discipulis eius et petro quia surrexit dominus alleluia.[36]]

clerici tipum mulierum gerentes[37]

Et tolla*n*t ~~mulieros~~ lintheam*i*na pro*c*eda*ntqu*e ad *p*opulu*m* clara voce can*t*an*t*es

Victime pas*ch*ali[38] [laudes immolant christiani.
Agnus redemit oues christus innocens patri reconciliauit peccatores.
Mors et vita duello conflixere mirando dux vite mortuus regnat viuus.
Dic nobis maria quid vidisti in via:
sepulcrum christi viuentis et gloriam vidi resurgentis.
Angelicos testes sudarium et vestes
surrexit christus spes nostra precedet suos in galyleam.
Credendum est magis soli marie veraci
quam iudeorum turbe fallaci.[39]
Scimus christum surrexisse a mortuis vere
tu nobis victor rex miserere alleluia.[40]]

hiis finit*is* incipit *c*antor

------

[35]Expansion of incipit of *Venite and videte* from LC Q3^r-Q3^v; cf. AS III, 236.

[36]Expansion of incipit of *Cito euntes* from BrL II, Pt. 2, 390; see also AS III, 250 (variant of CAO 1813).

[37]Marginal notation. See Schmid; Lipphardt omits.

[38]Lipphardt: pascali; Schmid: paschali.

[39]This unpleasant anti-Semitic stanza is omitted in LU 780.

[40]Expansion of incipit of *Victime paschali* from BrL II, Pt. 2, 375-76; for music, see LU 780.

Te deum [laudamus: te Dominum confitemur.
Te aeternum Patrem omnis terra veneratur.
Tibi omnes Angeli, tibi Caeli et universae Potestates:
Tibi Cherubim et Seraphim incessabili voce proclamant:
Sanctus: Sanctus: Sanctus Dominus Deus Sabaoth.
Pleni sunt caeli et terra majestatis gloriae tuae.
Te gloriosus Apostolorum chorus:
Te Prophetarum laudabilis numerus:
Te Martyrum candidatus laudat exercitus.
Te per orbem terrarum sancta confitetur Ecclesia:
Patrem immensae majestatis:
Venerandum tuum verum, et unicum Filium:
Sanctum quoque Paraclitum Spiritum.
Tu Rex gloriae, Christe.
Tu Patris sempiternus es Filius.
Tu ad liberandum suscepturus hominem,
non horruisti Virginis uterum.
Tu devicto mortis aculeo, aperuisti credentibus regna caelorum.
Tu ad dexteram Dei sedes, in gloria Patris.
Judex crederis esse venturus.
Te ergo quaesumus, tuis famulis subveni, quos pretioso sanguine redemisti.
Aeterna fac cum Sanctis tuis in gloria numerari.
Salvum fac populum tuum Domine, et benedic hereditati tuae.
Et rege eos, et extolle illos usque in aeternum.
Per singulos dies, benedicimus te.
Et laudamus nomen tuum in saeculorum, et in saeculum saeculi.
Dignare Domine die isto sine peccato nos custodire.
Miserere nostri Domine, miserere nostri.
Fiat misericordia tua Domine super nos, quemadmodum speravimus in te.
In te Domine speravi non confundar in aeternum.[41]]

conpulsatis interim omnis signis postea non dicitur versiculus nec Deus in adiutorium sed statim imponitur antiphona super laudes

----

[41]LU 1832-34.

et sic reuertu*n*tur ad chor*um*

Ad laud*es*

*a*ntiphon*a*. Angelus [autem domini descendit de celo et accedens reuoluit lapidem et sedebat super eum alleluia alleluia.[42]]

ELEVATION OF THE CROSS and VISIT TO THE SEPULCHER

In the holy night of Resurrection Sunday at the elevation of the cross this antiphon should be sung:

(*scratched out*)

The Lord, who for our sake hung upon the tree, is risen from the grave. Alleluia, alleluia, alleluia.

With the verses:

When Christ arose from the grave,
returning as a victor from hell,
he forcibly chained the tyrant
and opened paradise again.

Creator of all, we pray you,
in this Easter joy,
protect your people
from all the onslaughts of death.

Glory to you, Lord,
who have risen from the dead,
with the Father and Holy Spirit,

---

[42]Expansion of incipit of *Angelus autem Domine* from BrL II, Pt. 2, 376; for music, see LC R1ᵛ (CAO 1408).

world without end.

Then follows:

When Christ the king of glory, to vanquish hell, entered and overturned the gates of hell's kingdom, with the angel choir before him, those holy ones who were held captive in death cried out with tearful voice, "You have come, desired of nations, for whom we in chains have waited in darkness to lead us this night from prison. Our sighs cried out, the great laments reached up to you. You have become the hope of the desolate, the great consolation of those in torment. Alleluia."

Then at Matins:

Antiphon. Lord, open my lips, and my mouth shall show forth your praise.

Introit. O God, make speed to save me: O Lord, make haste to help me. Let them be confounded and put to shame who seek after my soul.
Glory to the Father and to the Son and to the Holy Spirit. As it was in the beginning, is now, and ever shall be, world without end. Amen.

Invitatory. Alleluia, alleluia, alleluia.

At Nocturn, the antiphon [is sung]:

I am who am, and my counsel is not with the ungodly: but my delight is in the law of the Lord, alleluia.

Psalm 1. Blessed is the man who has not walked in the counsel of the ungodly,
nor stood in the way of sinners, nor sat in the chair of pestilence.
But his will is in the law of the Lord,
and on his law he shall meditate day and night.

And he shall be like a tree which is planted near the running waters,
which shall bring forth its fruit, in due season.
And his leaf shall not fall off:
and all whatsoever he shall do shall prosper.
Not so the wicked, not so:
but they are like the dust, which the wind drives from the face of the earth.
Therefore the wicked shall not rise again in judgment:
nor sinners in the council of the just.
For the Lord knows the way of the just:
and the way of the wicked shall perish.

Antiphon. I have asked my father, alleluia, and he has given me the nations as my heritage, alleluia.

Psalm 2. Why have the Gentiles raged,
and the people devised vain things?
The kings of the earth stood up, and the princes met together,
against the Lord, and against his Christ.
Let us break their bonds asunder:
and let us cast away their yoke from us.
He that dwells in heaven shall laugh at them:
and the Lord shall deride them.
Then shall he speak to them in his anger,
and trouble them in his rage.
But I am appointed king by him over Sion his holy mountain,
preaching his commandment.
The Lord has said to me: You are my son,
this day have I begotten you.
Ask of me, and I will give you the Gentiles for your inheritance,
And the utmost parts of the earth for your possession.
You shall rule them with a rod of iron,
and shall break them in pieces like a potter's vessel.
And now, O you kings, understand;
receive instruction, you that judge the earth.
Serve you the Lord with fear:

and rejoice unto him with trembling.
Embrace discipline, lest at any time the Lord be angry,
and you perish from the just way.
When his wrath shall be kindled in a short time,
blessed are all they that trust in him.

Antiphon. I have slept and have taken my rest, and I have risen up again because the Lord sustained me, alleluia, alleluia.

Psalm 3. Why, O Lord, are they multiplied that afflict me?
Many are they who rise up against me.
Many say to my soul:
There is no salvation for him in his God.
But you, O Lord, are my protector,
my glory, and the lifter up of my head.
I have cried to the Lord with my voice:
and he has heard me from his holy hill.
I have slept and have taken my rest:
and I have risen up, because the Lord has protected me.
I will not fear thousands of the people, surrounding me;
arise, O Lord; save me, O my God.
For you have struck all them who are my adversaries without cause:
you have broken the teeth of sinners.
Salvation is of the Lord:
and your blessing is upon your people.

Verse. Whom do you seek, woman? Alleluia.
Responsory. I seek the living among the dead. Alleluia.

The Gospel according to Mark.

[In that time] Mary Magdalene and Mary Jacobi and Salome bought spices, seeking to anoint the Lord. . . .

With commentary by Gregory.
Pope Gregory. [*Lesson I.*] You have heard, dearly beloved brothers,

how the holy women who had followed the Lord came with spices to the tomb, and how, since they loved him when he was alive, they planned to honor him, now that he had died, with proofs of their love.

Responsory. The angel of the Lord came down from heaven, and as he came closer, he rolled away the stone and sat upon it. And he said to the women, "Fear not. I know that you seek the crucified one. He is risen. Come and see the place where the Lord was laid, alleluia."

Verse. The angel of the Lord spoke to the women and said, "Whom do you seek? Is it not Jesus you seek? He is risen. Come and see the place where the Lord was laid, alleluia."

Lesson II. But this that they did signifies what the members of the holy Church should be doing. We must listen to what was done so that we may learn what to do to imitate those things. And we who believe in him who has died, if we are characterized by the good odor of virtue and by a reputation for good works, may be said to come to the sepulcher with sweet spices.

Responsory. The angel of the Lord spoke to the women and said, "Whom do you seek? Is it not Jesus you seek? He is risen. Come and see, alleluia, alleluia."
Verse. Behold, he goes before you into Galilee where you will see him, as he said. He is risen. Come and see, alleluia, alleluia.

Lesson III. However, the women who had brought spices saw the angels; thus souls, fragrant in their virtue, come to the vision of the celestial citizens as they are drawn toward the Lord by their holy desires. . . .

Responsory. When the sabbath had ended, Mary Magdalene and Mary the mother of James and Salome bought spices and came to anoint Jesus, alleluia, alleluia.

Verse. And indeed, early one sabbath morning they came to the grave at the rising of the sun and came to anoint Jesus, alleluia, alleluia. Glory to the Father and to the Son and to the Holy Spirit. As it was in the beginning, is now, and ever shall be, world without end. Amen.

Responsory, repeated. When the sabbath had ended, Mary Magdalene and Mary the mother of James and Salome bought spices. Thus they came to anoint Jesus, alleluia, alleluia.

On that night, however, there should be a more solemn procession of Jesus Christ's resurrection after the responsory "When the sabbath had ended."

So singing, they proceed to the sepulcher. After the singing of the responsory for the last time, the three clerics in copes representing the women come to the sepulcher with thurible and incense. Seated inside are two deacons in dalmatics as angels. In a low, soft voice those who stand outside begin the antiphon:

"Who will roll the stone away from the door of the tomb for us? Alleluia, alleluia."

Those who are seated inside respond in a clear, strong voice [with the] antiphon:

"Whom do you seek in the sepulcher?"

Those standing outside reply:

"Jesus of Nazareth."

Those inside respond:

"He is not here, but he is risen."

And they add:

"Come and see the place where the Lord was laid, alleluia."

Then they enter and cense the place.

The angels add:

"Go quickly and tell the disciples and Peter that the Lord is risen, alleluia."

The clergy acting the part of the women:

And [the women] should pick up the winding sheet and process toward the people, singing in a clear, strong voice:

To the paschal victim
Christians may offer praise.
The sheep are ransomed by the Lamb;
and the innocent Christ
has reconciled sinners to his Father.

The miraculous conflict of death and life
is ended;
the champion of life, though slain,
lives to reign.

Tell us, Mary,
what did you see on the way?
The tomb which the living enclosed;
I saw Christ's glory as he rose.

The angels there testified
as did the shroud with grave-clothes.
Christ, my hope, is risen:
he will go before you into Galilee.

The truthful Mary is more to be believed

than the untruthful crowd of Jews.[43]
We know that Christ is truly risen
from the dead:
Show us your mercy, victorious king.

At the end [of the preceding sequence], the cantor begins the Te Deum.

We praise you, God: we acknowledge you to be the Lord.
You are the eternal Father: the whole world worships you.
To you all the angels, the heavens, and all the Powers, Cherubim and Seraphim, proclaim aloud unceasingly,
"Holy, holy, holy Lord, God of Sabaoth.
Heaven and earth are full of the majesty of your glory."
The glorious company of the apostles, the laudable host of prophets, the white-clad band of martyrs praise you.
The holy Church throughout the whole earth confesses that you are the Father of unlimited majesty; true and worthy of honor, your only Son; also the holy Spirit, the comforter.
You are the king of glory, O Christ. You are the eternal Son of the Father.
When you came to liberate humans, you did not scorn the Virgin's womb.
You overcame the sting of Death: you opened the kingdom of heaven to all believers.
You are seated at the right hand of God, in the glory of the Father: we believe that you will come to be our judge.
We therefore ask that you come and help your people, whom you have redeemed with your precious blood.
Cause them to be counted with your saints in eternal glory.
Save your people, Lord, and bless your inheritance.
Rule them, and raise them up in eternity.
Daily we bless you and we praise your name, world without end.
Keep us, Lord, this day without sin.
Have mercy on us, Lord, have mercy on us.

---

[43]See footnote 39, above.

Let your mercy, Lord, be upon us, as we have trusted in you.
In you, Lord, have I trusted. I will never be confounded.

At the tolling of all the bells, afterwards the versicle "O God, make speed to save us" is not said. But the antiphon for Lauds occurs immediately, and they return to the choir.

At Lauds:

Antiphon: The angel of the Lord came down from heaven, and came and rolled away the stone, and sat upon it. Alleluia, alleluia.

7

Depositio Crucis and *Elevatio Crucis*
from a Vadstena Processional

MS. C. 506 in the Uppsala University Library is a Processional of the fifteenth century from the Brigittine double monastery at Vadstena in the Linköping diocese. It is parchment and possesses a brown leather cover, scarred, with the clasps missing. The notation is written in square notes on a four-line staff. The manuscript is clearly written by a Vadstena scribe, and present are the distinctive initials in red, blue, and black which identify the Vadstena manuscript style.[1] The dimensions are 22 x 14.8 cm.

While no *Visitatio* is present, the manuscript does contain, on folios 9v-11v, the *Depositio crucis*, celebrated on Good Friday and involving the burial of the cross (and, presumably, the Host), and the *Elevatio crucis*. The rubrics indicate that at Vadstena the cross was removed from the Easter sepulcher during the latter ceremony, celebrated on Easter Sunday before Matins in representation of the Resurrection. As noted above, there is no evidence concerning the location of the Easter sepulcher in the church at Vadstena, though the

---

[1]The manuscript style is similar, for example, to Uppsala Universitetbibliotek MS. 458, also written at Vadstena; see the pages from this manuscript illustrated in Andreas Lindblom, *Vadstena Klosters Öden* (Vadstena, 1973), p. 87.

design of the building prior to the expulsion of the Brigittine Order from Sweden in 1595 is well documented. These ceremonies, however, are specified as ones to be performed after the completion of the sisters' vespers, but it is not certain that these rites were done by them. If the sisters rather than the brothers had responsibility for the ceremonies, a portable Easter sepulcher in the nuns' gallery may be conjectured. Subsequent practice suggests a structure like a coffer tomb in which the cross or crucifix might be laid.

After the nuns fled from Sweden to Poland and later to Marienwater and Uden in North Brabant, Holland, they attempted to preserve their way of celebrating Good Friday, which until modern times involved the use of a corpus. Sister M. Patricia of the present cloister at Vadstena remembers the practice on Good Friday at Uden before the return of the Brigittine nuns to Vadstena. Following the *Improperia*, the sisters left the church to bring back into it in a procession the life-sized corpus which she describes as "terribly tortured and beautiful." The corpus was placed on a catafalque, and around it were placed candles and flowers. The corpus remained in the church for twenty hours, and then was returned to the monastery until the next year.[2] Similar figures survive from Brigittine houses in Maribo and Mariager, Denmark (fig. 3).[3]

---

[2]Interview with Sister M. Patricia, Sankta Birgittas Kloster, Vadstena, 29 June 1986.

[3]The Maribo corpus is in the National Museum Copenhagen. A woodcarving of Christ from a Swedish Easter sepulchre is also extant from Roslagsbro, Uppland; see Aron Andersson, *Medieval Wooden Sculpture in Sweden* (Stockholm: Almqvist & Wiksell International, 1980), III, 174-75, fig. 106. This figure, however, seems to have been atypical in its representation of the dead Christ (ibid., III, 175).

Walther Lipphardt has listed this set of ceremonies as No. 449a (Link[5]).

<DEPOSITIO CRUCIS et ELEVATIO CRUCIS>

In die par*asc*eues finitis uesp*eris* soror*um* qu*ando* crux portatur ad sepulchr*um*.

Responsorium Ecce q*u*omodo moritur iustus[1] et nemo percipit corde viri iusti tolluntur et nemo considerat a facie iniquitatis sublatus est iustus. Et erit in pace memoria eius.[2]

Versus In pace factus est[3] locus e l ius et in syon habitacio eius. Et e[rit in pace memoria eius].[4]

[*Antiphona.*] Caro mea requiescet in spe.[5]

[*Antiphona.*] In pace factus est locus eius et in syon habitacio eius. [Et erit in pace memoria eius.[6]]

In reditu de sepul*c*ro

[*Responsorium.*] Sepulto domino signatu*m* est[7] monumentum voluentes lapidem ad ostiu*m* monumenti. Ponentes milites qui custodirent[8] l illud.[9]

Versus. In pace factus est locus eius et in syon habitacio eius. [Et erit in pace memoria eius].

---

[1]Lipphardt omits the remainder of the text of *Ecce quomodo moritur*.

[2]Cf. BrL II, Pt. 2, 372; LU 767-68 (CAO 6605).

[3]Lipphardt omits the remainder of the text of *In pace factus est*.

[4]Cf. BrL II, Pt. 2, 372.

[5]Cf. BrL II, Pt. 2, 371; LU 753 (CAO 1775).

[6]CAO 6605; cf. BrL II, Pt. 2, 372, and LU 769.

[7]Lipphardt omits the remainder of the text of *Sepulto domino signatum est*.

[8]At this point in the manuscript, a rubric refers to *Inventor rutili*; for the rubric and the hymn, see the Appendix, below. However, this item clearly does not belong at this point, and the rubric is misplaced.

[9]Cf. BrL. II, Pt. 2, 371; for music, see LU 773, the notation of which is similar but not identical to the version given in this manuscript.

In die pasche q*uando* crux leuat*ur.*

Surrexit dominus de sepulcro qui pro nobis pependit in ligno alleluya.

Cum surgit *christus* [tumulo
victor redit de baratro[10]
tirannum[11] trudens vinculo,
et reserans paradisum.]

Q*uesumu*s auctor o*mniu*m,
[in hoc paschali gaudio
ab omni mortis impetu
tuum defendas[12] populum.]

Glo*ri*a tibi do*mine*[13]
q*ui s*urrexisti [a mortuis,
*cum patre et sancto spiritu
in sempiterna secula. Amen.*[14]]

Item an*tifona.* Cum rex glorie *chr*istus infernu*m* debellaturus intraret et chorus angelicus an|te faciem eius portas principi*um* tolli preciperet sanctoru*m* populus qui tenebatur in morte captiuus voce lacrimabili clamaueru*nt* aduenisti desiderabilis que*m* expectabamus in tenebris vt educeres hac nocte vinculatos de claustris te nostra vocabant suspiria te larga require|bant lamenta tu factus es spes desolatis magna consolacio in tormentis. Alleluya.

---

[10]*Analecta Hymnica*: barathro.

[11]*Analecta Hymnica*: tyrannum.

[12]*Analecta Hymnica*: defende.

[13]The abbreviation *q.v.* is entered after the words *Gla tibi do.*

[14]Expansion of incipit of *Ad cenam agni prouidi* from BrL, Pt. 2, 387.

DEPOSITION OF THE CROSS and ELEVATION OF THE CROSS

After the sisters' Vespers on Good Friday, as the cross is carried to the sepulcher:

Responsory. Behold, how the righteous man dies and no one gives heed in his heart. Just men are lifted up and no one considers it. The just man is offered up in the face of wickedness. And his memory will endure in peace.

Verse. His abode is established in peace and in Sion is his dwelling place. And his memory will endure in peace.

[*Antiphon.*] My flesh shall rest in hope.

[*Antiphon.*] His abode is established in peace and in Sion is his dwelling place. And his memory will endure in peace.

On returning from the sepulcher:

Responsory. When the Lord had been entombed, they sealed the grave, rolling a stone across the door of the grave. And they set soldiers there to guard it.

Verse. His abode is established in peace and in Sion is his dwelling place. And his memory will endure in peace.

On Easter Day at the Elevation of the Cross:

The Lord, who for our sakes hung upon the tree, is risen from the grave.

When Christ arose from the grave,
returning as a victor from hell,
he forcibly chained the tyrant
and opened paradise again.

Creator of all, we pray you,
in our Easter joy,
protect your people
from all the onslaughts of death.

Glory to you, Lord,
who have risen from the dead,
with the Father and the Holy Spirit,
world without end.

Antiphon. When Christ the king of glory, to vanquish hell, entered and overturned the gates of hell's kingdom, with the angel choir before him, those holy ones who were held captive in death cried out with tearful voice, "You have come, desired of nations, for whom we in chains have waited in darkness to lead us this night from prison. Our sighs cried out, the great laments reached up to you. You have become the hope of the desolate, the great consolation of those in torment. Alleluia."

APPENDIX: *INVENTOR RUTILI*

Inserted in No. 7 at the bottom of the page after the word *custodirent* in *Sepulto domino* is a rubric referring to *Inuentor rutili*. The rubric and the hymn, which appears on fol. b viii, are as follows:

In vigilia pasche post benediccionem ignis Inuentor rutili. Require infra in quinto folio. b viii.

Inuentor rutili dux bone luminis
qui certis vicibus tempora diuidis
merso sole chaos ingruit horridum
lumen[15] redde tuis *christe* fidelibus.

---

[15]*Analecta Hymnica*: lucem.

Quamuis innumero sydere regiam
lunarique polum lampade pinxeris
incussu silicis lumina nos tamen n̶
monstras saxigeno semine querere.

Nesciret[16] | [homo spem sibi luminis
In Christi solido corpore conditam,
Qui dici stabilem se voluit petram,
Nostris igniculis unde genus venit.

Pinguis quos olei rore madentibus
Lychnis aut facibus pascimus aridis,
Quin et fila favis scirpea floreis
Presso melle prius conlita fingimus.

Vivax flamma viget, seu cava testula
Succum linteolo suggerit ebrio,
Seu pinus piceam fert alimoniam,
Seu ceram teretem stuppa calens bibit.

Nectar de liquido vertice fervidum
Guttatim lacrimis stillat olentibus,
Ambustum quoniam vis facit ignea
Imbrem de madido flere cacumine.

Splendent ergo tuis muneribus, pater,
Flammis mobilibus scilicet atria,
Absentemque diem lux agit aemula,
Quam nox cum lacero victa fugit peplo.

Sed quis non rapidi luminis arduam
Manantemque Deo cernat originem,
Moyses nempe Deum spinifera in rubo
Vidit conspicuo lumine flammeum.

---

[16]*Analecta Hymnica*: Ne nesciret. At this point the hymn breaks off; as noted above, the hymn is incomplete because the adjacent leaves are missing from the manuscript.

O res digna, Deus, quam tibi roscidae
Noctis principio grex tuus offerat!
Lucem, qua tribuis nil pretiosius,
Lucem, qua reliqua praemia cernimus.

Tu lux vera oculis, lux quoque sensibus,
Intus tu speculum, tu speculum foris,
Lumen, quod famulans offero, suscipe
Tinctum paciferi chrismatis unguine.

Per Christum genitum, summe pater, tuum,
In quo visibilis stat tibi gloria,
Qui noster Dominus, qui tuus unicus
Spirat de patrio corde paraclitum.

Per quem splendor, honor, laus, sapientia,
Maiestas, bonitas et pietas tua
Regnum continuat numine triplici
Texens perpetuis saecula saeculis.[17]]

TRANSLATION

On Easter Even, after the blessing of the fire, [the hymn] Inuentor
rutili *[is sung]; see further in quinto folio b viii.*

Author of roseate light, good Prince,
who divides all time in set array,
once the sun descends, savage chaos strikes.
Restore your light, O Christ, to your faithful.

With numberless stars you have adorned your court
and the panoply of heaven with lunar torch.
Yet at the striking of a flint,
you teach us to seek lights born of stone.

---

[17]Completion of *Inuentor rutili* from *Analecta Hymnica.*

Number Seven

Lest man not know the hope of light
founded on the solid body of Christ,
he chose to be called the steady rock
from which, down to our small lights, comes our race.

We supply fat in drops of oil
to moistened lamp or arid firebrands.
Indeed, we mould rushen threads from flowery honeycomb
by first pressing out the honey smearing them.

The living flame thrives; either a hollow earthen lamp
carries the draught to a wick
or the pine gives up its sustaining pitch
or glowing flax drinks smooth wax.

Fiery nectar drips, drop by drop, in oily tears
from the flickering coil of flame,
whereas the fiery force produces a shower
from the burning pinnacle.

They shine there by your bounty, O Father,
with swaying flames like forecourts.
The emulous light creates the absent day,
which vanquished night, with mangled robe, now flees.

Yet who does not discern within the light's swift flight
the lofty and enduring authorship of God.
Moses, indeed, saw God in a burning bush,
aflame in visible light.

How worthy, God, the service which your flock offers you
in the dewy beginnings of the night:
the light, than which nothing more precious is given—
the light, by which we discern all other gifts.

You are the true light of the eye and the light of the senses
within, a mirror and without, a mirror.

Number Seven

The light which I in service offer, then accept,
moistened with the peace-bearing oil of chrism.

Through Christ your Son, great Father,
in whom glory becomes visible.
he, our Lord, he, your sole begotten,
breathes from the Father's heart the Paraclete.

Through him be splendor, honor, praise, wisdom,
Majesty, goodness, and graciousness.
May his kingdom endure in threefold sway,
weaving the ages into unending ages.

Musical Transcriptions

No. 2. VISITATIO SEPULCHRI

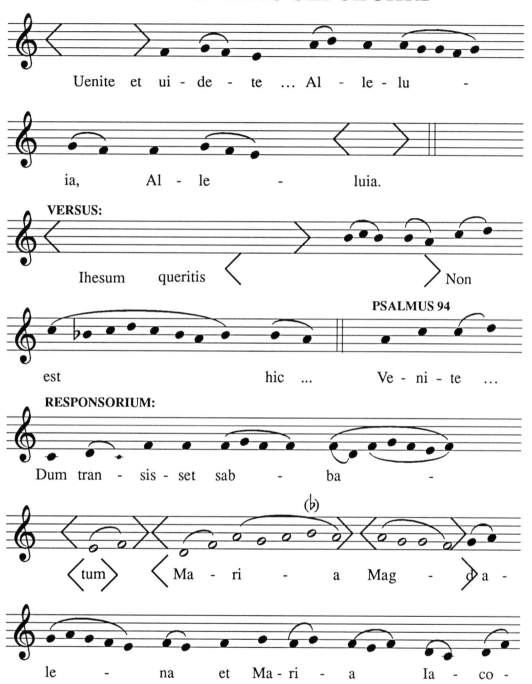

Uenite et ui - de - te ... Al - le - lu -

ia,   Al - le - luia.

VERSUS:

Ihesum   queritis   Non

PSALMUS 94

est   hic ...   Ve - ni - te ...

RESPONSORIUM:

Dum tran - sis - set sab - ba -

tum   Ma - ri - a Mag - da -

le - na et Ma - ri - a Ia - co -

bi   et   Sa - lo - me   -   e   e - me -

runt   a - ro - ma   -   ta,   ut

ue   -   ni - en   -   tes   un - ge   -   rent

Ie   -   sum.   Al   -   le - lu   -   ia,

Al   -   le   -

lu   -   ia.

VERSUS:

Et   ual - de   m   a   -   ne   u -

na sa - ba - to - rum ue - ni - unt ad mo -

nu - men - tum or - to iam

so - le. Ut ue - ni -

en - tes un - ge - rent

Ie - sum. Al - le - lu - ia,

Al - le - (le) -

lu - ia. Glo - ri - a [Patri...]

Dum tran - sis - set sab - ba -

tum Ma - ri - a Mag - da -

le - na et Ma - ri - a Ia - co -

bi et Sa - lo - me - e e - me -

runt a - ro - ma - ta, ut

ue - ni - en - tes un - ge - rent

Ie - sum. Al - le - lu - ia,

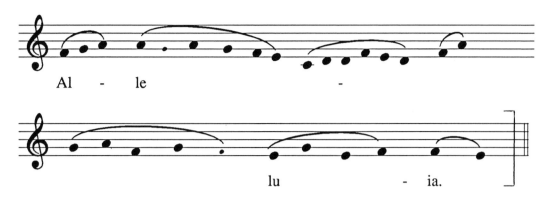

Al - le - lu - ia.

(Interpolated notes in *Dum transisset* are taken from *Antiphonale Sarisburiense,* III, 235-236.)

SIC CANTANTES PROCEDUNT AD SEPULCRUM ET STANT FORIS EXPECTANTES. ET ECCE TRES CLERICI PRO MULIERIBUS IN CAPPIS UENIUNT AD SEPULCRUM CUM TURRIBULIS SEDENTIBUS INTRO DUOBUS DIACONIBUS CUM DALMATICIS PRO ANGELIS, ET SIC INCIPIENT EXTRA STANTES:

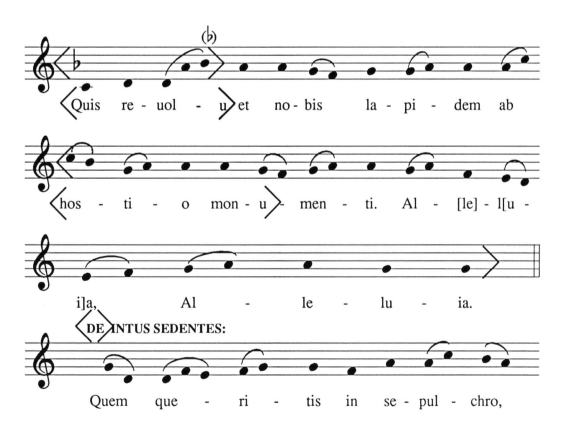

Quis re-uol-u-et no-bis la-pi-dem ab hos-ti-o mon-u-men-ti. Al-[le]-l[u-i]a, Al-le-lu-ia.

DE INTUS SEDENTES:

Quem que-ri-tis in se-pul-chro,

O Chris - ti - co - le?

ITEM EXTRA STANTES:

Ihe - sum Na - za - re - num O ce - li - co - le.

(Interpolated notes are taken from No. 5.)

DEINTUS SEDENTES RESPONDENT:

Non est hic, sur - re - xit e - nim si - cut

pre - di - xe - rat. I - te nun - ci - a - te

qui - a sur - re - xit Ie - sus.

ET ADDUNT:

Ue - ni - te et ui - de - te lo - cum u - bi po-

si - tus e - rat Do - mi-nus, Al - le - lu - ia, Al - le - lu - ia.

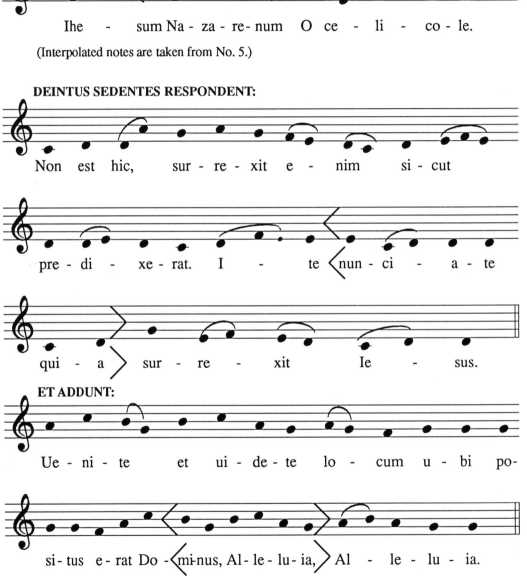

TUNC INTRANT TURIFICANTES LOCUM ET ADDUNT ANGELI:

Ci- to   e - un - tes   di - ci - te   di - sci - pu - lis

qui a sur - re - xit   Do-mi-nus,   Al - le - lu - ia.

ET TOLLUNT MARIE LINTHEAMINA PROCEDUNT AD POPULUM, CANTANTES:

Sur - re- xit   Do - mi - nus   de

se-   pul-   chro   qui   pro   no -   bis   pe -

pen-   dit   in li - gno. Al- le- lu- ia,   Al-   le- lu - ia.

(Interpolated notes in *Cito euntes* and *Surrexit Dominus* are taken from *Antiphonale Sarisburiense*, III, 250.)

Te De- um lau- da- mus: te Do-

mi - num con - fi - te- mur. Te ae - ter - num

Pa- trem om - nis ter - ra ve - ne - ra-

tur. Ti- bi om - nes An- ge- li, ti -

bi Cae - li et u - ni - ver - sae Po - tes- ta-

tes: Ti- bi Che - ru - bim et Se- ra- phim

in ces- sa - bi - li vo - ce pro- cla- mant:

Sanc - tus: Sanc - tus:

Sanc - tus Do - mi - nus De - us Sa -

ba- oth. Ple- ni sunt cae - li et ter - ra ma-

jes- ta - tis glo - ri - ae tu - ae. Te

glo - ri - o- sus A - pos - to - lo - rum cho-

rus: Te Pro - phe - ta- rum lau - da - bi -

lis nu - me- rus: Te Mar - ty - rum can - di-

Tu Pa- tris Sem - pi - ter - nus es Fi - li - us.

Tu ad li - be - ran-dum su - scep - tu-rus ho -

mi - nem, non hor- ru - is-ti Vir- gi - nis

u - te - rum. Tu de- vic - to mor - tis a - cu -

le- o, a - pe- ru - is - ti cre - den - ti - bus

re- gna cae- lo - rum. Tu ad dex - te - ram

De - i se- des, in glo- ri - a Pa - tris.

Ju - dex cre - de - ris es - se ven - tu - rus.

Te er - go quae - su - mus, tu - is fa - mu - lis sub -

ve - ni, quos pre - ti - o - so san - gui - ne re -

de - mi - sit. Ae - ter - na fac cum Sanc - tis

tu - is in glo - ri - a nu - me - ra - ri.

Sal - vum fac po - pu - lum tu - um Do - mi - ne,

et be - ne - dic he - re - di - ta - ti tu -

ae. Et re- ge e - os, et ex- tol-

le il - los us - que in ae - ter- num. Per

sing- u - los di- es, be - ne- di - ci-

mus te. Et lau- da - mus no - men tu- um in sae-

cu- lum, et in sae- cu - lum sae - cu - li.

Di - gna- re Do - mi - ne di - e i- sto

si - ne pec - ca - to nos cu - sto- di - re. Mi-

se - re - re no - stri Do - mi - ne, mi -

se - re - re no - stri. Fi - at mi - se - ri -

cor - di - a tu - a Do - mi - ne su - per

nos, quem - ad - mo - dum spe - ra - vi - mus in te.

In te Do - mi - ne spe - ra - vi:

non con - fun - dar in ae - ter - num.

(Following the incipit, the music for the *Te Deum* is taken from the *Liber Usualis*, pp. 1832-34.)

No. 3. VISITATIO SEPULCHRI

IN DIE PASCE

Qvis re - oul - uat no - bis la - pi - dem ab os - ti - o mo - nu - men - ti? Al - le - lu - ia, Al - le - lu - ia. Quem que - ri - tis in se - pul - chro, O Christi co - le? Ihe - sum Na - za - re - num cru - ci - fi - xum, O ce - li - co - le. Non est hic. Sur - re - xit si - cut pre - di - xe - ram i - te nun - ci -

a - te quia sur- re - xit a mor - te.

Ve - ni - te et ui - de - te lo- cum u - bi

positus e - rat Do - mi - nus. Al -

le- lu - ia, Al- le - lu - ia. Sur - re-

xit Dominus de se- pul - chro

qui pro no- bis pe- pen- dit in li - gn o Alleluia.

Deus qui pro nobis filium tuum crucis patib<ulum> subire uoluisti, et inimici a nobis expelleres postestatem concede nobis famulis tuis, ut in resurrectionis eius gaudiis semper uiuamus. Per Dominum nostrum Christum.

No. 5. VISITATIO SEPULCHRI

...PRO ANGELIS SICQUE SUBMISSA UOCE QUI EXTRA STANT INCIPIUNT ANTIPHONAM:

Ma - ri - a Mag - da - le - na et a - li -

a Ma - ri - a fe - re - bant di - lu - cu - lo

a - ro - ma - ta Do -

mi - num que - ren - tes in mo - nu -

EXTRA STANTES INCIPIENT HANC ANTIPHONAM:

men - to. Quis re - uol - uit no - bis ab

hos - ti - o la - pi - dem quem te - ge - re

sanc - tum cer - ni - mus se -

141

pul-chrum.　　Quem　　que-　　ri　-　　tis,　O　tre-

mu-　le　mu-　li-　e　-　res　in　hoc　tu　-

EXTRA STANTES ANTIPHONAM:

mu　-　lo　plo　-　ran-　tes?　Ihe-　sum　Na　-　za　-　re　-　num

ANGELIS HANC ANTIPHONAM:

cru　-　ci　-　fi-　xum　que-　ri　-　mus.　　Non

est　hic　quem　que　-　ri　-　tis　sed　sci　-　to　e　-

un　-　tes　nun　-　ti　-　a　-　te　di　-　sci-　pu　-　lis　e　-

ius　et　Pe　-　tro　qui　-　a　sur　-　re　-　xit

ANTIPHONAM:

Ihe- sus. Ue - ni - te et ui - de - te

lo- cum u - bi po - si - tus e - rat Do - mi - nus,

MULIERES ISTAM
ANTIPHONAM:

Al - le- lu - ia, Al- le - lu - ia. Ad mo -

nu- men - tum ue - ni - mus ge - men- tes an -

ge- lum Do - mi - ni se - den - tem ui - di - mus

et di - cen- tem qui - a sur - re - xit

ANTIPHONAM:

Ihe - sus. Cur - re - bant du - o si - mul et

143

il - le al - li - us di - sci - pu - lus pre -

cu - cur - rit ci - ci - us Pe - tro et ue - nit

pri - or ad mo - nu - men - tum, Al - le -

ANTIPHONAM:

lu - ia. Cer - ni - tis, O so - ci - i, ec -

ce lin - the - a - mi - na et su - da - ri -

um et cor - pus non est in - uen - tum.

ANTIPHONAM:

Sur - re - xit Do - mi - nus de

144

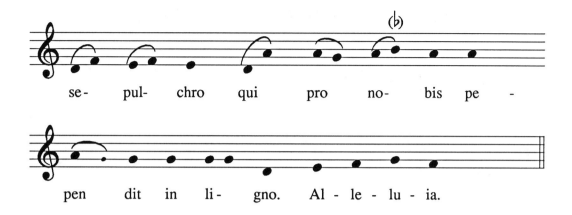

se- pul- chro qui pro no- bis pe -

pen dit in li- gno. Al - le - lu - ia.

No. 7. DEPOSITIO CRUCIS and ELEVATIO CRUCIS

IN DIE PARASCEUES FINITIS VESPERIS SORORUM QUANDO CRUX PORTATUR AD SEPULCHRUM

RESPONSORIUM:

Ec- ce quo-mo-do mo - ri - tur iu-

stus, et ne- mo per - ci - pit

cor- de; vi - ri iu - sti tol - lun-

tur, et ne- mo con- si -

de- rat. A fa- ci - e i-

ni - qui- ta- tis sub - la- tus

est ius- tus, Et

e - rit in pa- ce me-

VERSUS:

mo- ri - a e - ius. In pa - ce

fac- tus est lo-

cus e - ius et in Si - on ha - bi-

ta - ti - o e -

ius. Et e - rit in pa-

147

ce me- mo- ri- a e- ius.

ANTIPHONAM:

Ca - ro me- a re- qui - e - scet in spe.

In pa - ce fac - tus est lo- cus e- ius et

in Si- on ha - bi - ta- ti - o e - ius.

RESPONSORIUM IN REDITU SEPULCHRUM:

Se - pul - to Do- mi- no, si - gna - tum est

mo - nu - men- tum, vol- uen- tes

la - pi- dem ad o - sti - um

mo - nu - men- ti: Po - nen -

tes mi - li - tes, qui cu - sto - di -

rent il - lud. In pa -

ce fac- tus est lo - cus e - ius, et

in Si- on ha - bi - ta - ti - o

IN DIE PASCHE, QUANDO CRUX LEVATUR:

e - ius. Sur - re - xit Do-

mi - nus de se- pul- chro qui pro no -

bis pe- pen- dit in li- gno. Al - le- lu - ia.

Cum sur - git Chris - tus tu - mu - lo vic - tor

re - dit de ba - ra- thro, ty - ran- num tru - dens vin -

cu- lo, et re- se - rans pa - ra- di- sum.

Que - su - mus auc - tor om - ni - um, in hoc

pa - scha - li gau - di- o ab om - ni mor - tis im -

pe- tu tu - um de - fen - de po - pu- lum.

Glo - ri - a ti - bi, Do - mi - ne, qui sur-

re - xi - sti a mor - tu- is, cum Pa - tre et Sanc -

to Spi - ri - tu in sem- pi - ter- na sae - cu-

la. A - men.

Cum rex glo- ri - e Chri-

stus in - fer - num de - bel - la - tu - rus

in - tra- ret, et cho - rus

an - ge- li - cus an - te fa -

ci - em e- ius por- tas prin- ci - pium tol-

li pre- ci- pe- ret, sanc - to - rum po -

pu- lus, qui te - ne - ba - tur in mor - te

cap – ti - uus, ec - ce la - cri -

ma – bi - li cla - ma - ue - runt: Ad - ue -

ni – sti de - si - de - ra – bi - lis, quem

ex - pec - ta - ba - mus in te - ne - bris,

ut e - du - ce - res hac noc - te vin - cu -

la - tos de clau - stris. Te no - stra

vo - ca - bant su - spi - ri - a, te

lar - ga re - qui - re - bant

la - men - ta. Tu fac - tus es

spes de - so - la - tis, ma - gna

153

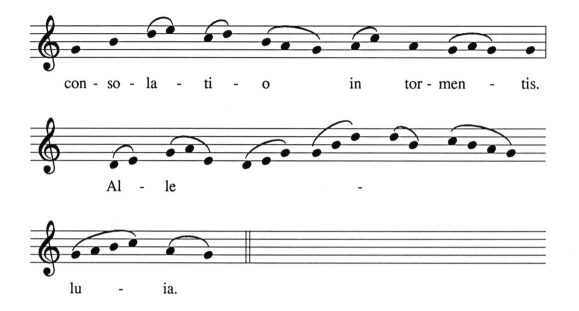

con - so - la - ti - o   in   tor - men - tis.

Al - le -

lu - ia.

In - uen - tor ru - ti - li, dux bo - ne, lu - mi-

nis, Qui cer - tis vi - ci - bus tem - po - ra di -

ui - dis, Mer - so so - le cha - os in- gru - it

hor - ri - dum, lu - men red- de tu - is, Chri - ste, fi -

de - li - bus, Quam- uis in- nu - me - ro sy - de-

re re - gi- am Lu - na - ri- que po - lum lam-

pa - de pin - xe- ris, In - cus - so si - li - cis lu-

155

mi - na nos ta - men Mon- stras sa- xi - ge - no

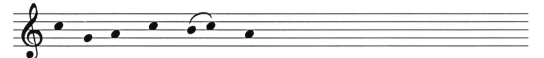

se - mi - ne que - re - re.

Index

Index

Index

2. The Visit of the Holy Women to the Sepulcher. Linköping Cathedral.

1. Easter Sepulcher in north wall of chancel. Kiaby, Skåne.

3. Sepulcher with corpus formerly used in Good Friday and Easter ceremonies. c. 1500. Mariager, Denmark.

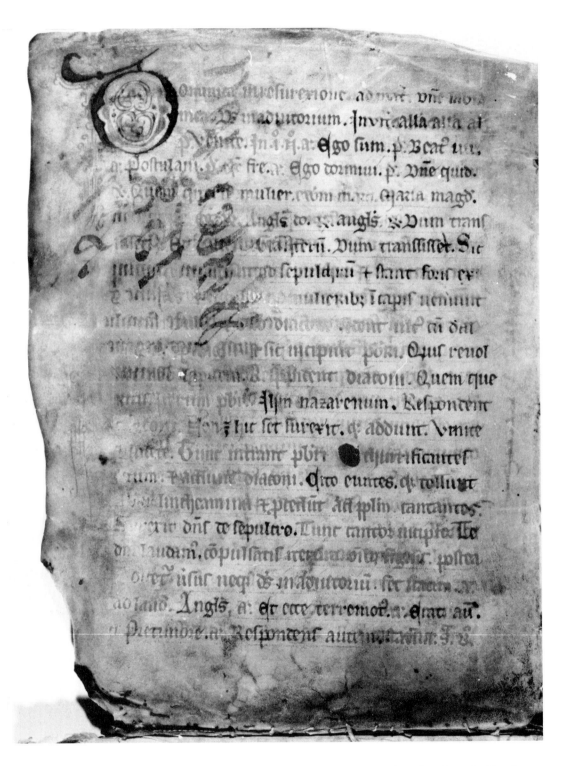

4. Matins and *Visitatio Sepulchri* (No. 1) in fragment of Linköping Ordinal (Riksarkivet, Värmland, 1589, No. 12).

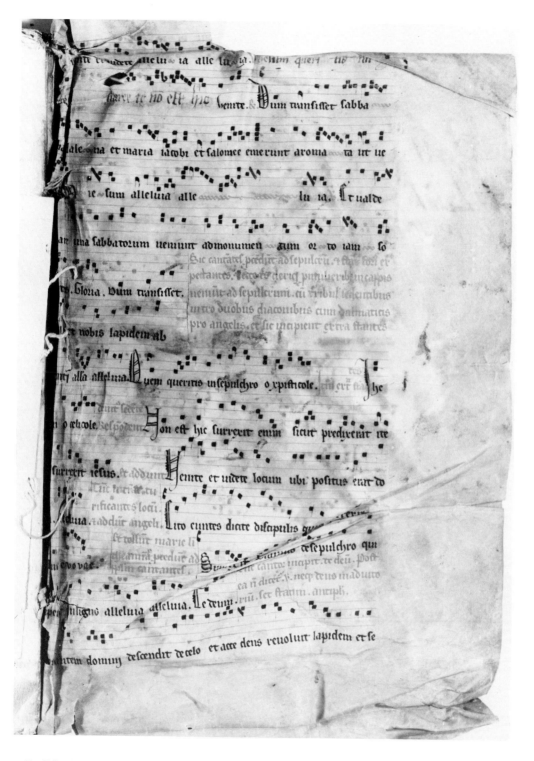

5. Matins (incomplete) and *Visitatio Sepulchri* (No. 2) in fragment of Linköping Antiphonal (Riksarkivet, Småland 1574, No. 3:2).

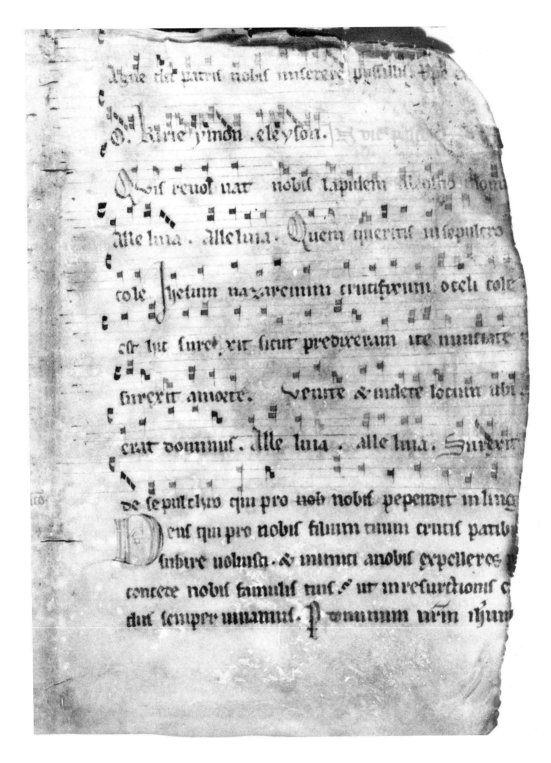

6. *Visitatio Sepulchri* (No. 3) from a Gradual possibly from the Stockholm area (Riksarkivet, Dalarna 1575, No. 14).

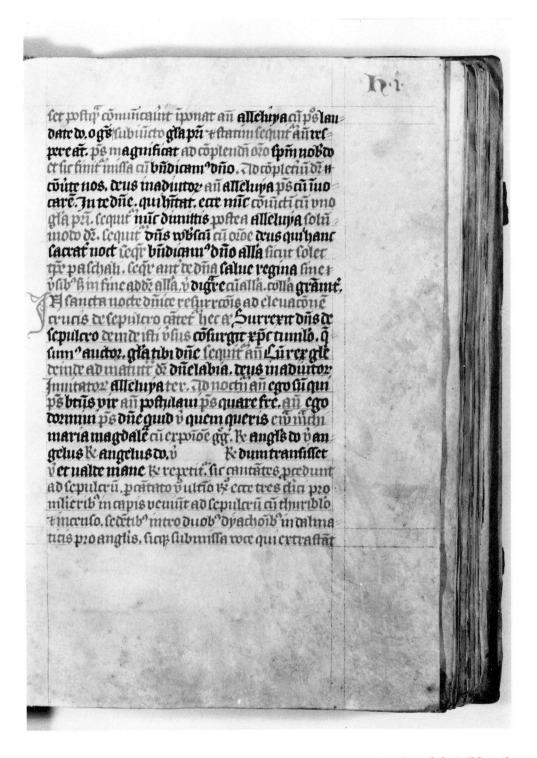

7. Beginning of Matins, *Elevatio Crucis*, and *Visitatio Sepulchri* (No. 4) from a Vadstena Ordinal (Riksarkivet, Skoklostersammlingen, No. 2 [E 8899], p. hi).

incipiēt añ **quis reuoluet** r̄ūdēt clara voce de
uirtus sedētes añ **que queritis** Itē extra stātes
ibm **nazareñ** r̄ūdēt dcūt⁹ **non est hic** ⁊ addūt
venite et videte tūc intrēt ⁊ thurificēt locū. addūtq̄
angli **ecce eūtes** ⁊ tollant milieres lintexmia pro
cedātq̄ ad p̄lm clara wce cātātes **victime pascha-**
li laudes hijs finitis incipit cantor **Te dm** cōpul-
satis interim ōib⁹ signis. postea nō dr̄ v̄ n̄ dr̄s mag-
uitor. ß stati imponit añ ad laudes et sic reuūt ad
choꝛ. Ad laudes añ **Angelus aūt dm** añ **et ecce ter-**
re motus añ **erat aūte** añ **pre timore** añ **r̄ūdēs at**
addat stati ℞ b̄ūdes añ **et valde mane** seqr̄ dūs
vobiscū cū oꝛōe **deus qui hodierna die per vnige-**
nitū ℞ p̄mam **deus in adiutoꝛ** statim añ **angelus at**
p̄s **deus in noīe Confitem̄**. v̄t ūacdati. retribue
quiacūq̄ infra hanc ebdōam nō dr̄ ß post p̄s **Hec**
hec dies sine v̄ū ⁊ alleluya cū nemna ⁊ statim
dūs vobiscū collcā dc⁹ **qui hod⁹ die** Ad tciā añ **et ecce**
ce terre motus ℞ ⁊ cetaut̄s. Ad vi añ **erat**
autem ℞ tc̄ut̄s. dente b̄ūdr̄ aqua ⁊ aspergit
cū añ **vidi aquā** p̄s **confitemī** Ad pcessionē a cū
rer gl̄e v̄sus fortunati **Salue festa dies**. ad stacō-
nem ℞ **sedit angelus** v̄ crucifixū cū repticōne
nolite metuere v̄ recordamī cū alleluya redit
in choꝛ. Seqr̄ collcā **Omipoñs sempr̄ne** Ad missā
offm **Resurrexi ⁊ adhuc** p̄s **dñe pbasti** Collecta

8. Conclusion of Matins, *Elevatio Crucis,* and *Visitatio Sepulchri* (No. 4)
from a Vadstena Ordinal (Riksarkivet, Skoklostersammlingen, No. 2 [E
8899], p. hii).

9. Beginning of *Visitatio Sepulchri* (No. 5) from a Linköping Breviary (Riks-arkivet, Älfsborg/Lödöse, 1575-81).

10. Conclusion of *Visitatio Sepulchri* (No. 5) from a Linköping Breviary (Riksarkivet, Älfsborg/Lödöse, 1575-81).

11. Beginning of Matins, *Elevatio Crucis*, and *Visitatio Sepulchri* (No. 6) from a Linköping Ordinal (1493) (Uppsala Universitets Biblioteket, MS. C. 428, fol. 37r).

12. Conclusion of Matins, *Elevatio Crucis*, and *Visitatio Sepulchri* (No. 6) from a Linköping Ordinal (1493) (Uppsala Universitets Biblioteket, MS. C. 428, fol. 37ᵛ).

13. Beginning of *Depositio Crucis* and *Elevatio Crucis* (No. 7) from a Vadstena Processional (Uppsala Universitets Biblioteket, MS. C. 506, fol. b ii [9ᵛ]).

ius et in syon habita cio e ius.

Et e. Caro mea requiescet in spe.

In pace factus est locus eius et in syon

habitacio eius. (In reditu de se pulc̄) Sepulto domino

signatū est monumen tum voluentes

lapi dem ad ostiū monumen ti. Po

nentes mili tes qui custodi rent

In vigilia pasche post b̄ndc̄oēm ignis Iuuetor cūūli. Reqēre infra in qūto folio. b viii

14. Continuation of *Depositio Crucis* and *Elevatio Crucis* (No. 7) from a Vadstena Processional (Uppsala Universitets Biblioteket, MS. C. 506, fol. b ii [10ʳ]).

15. Continuation of *Depositio Crucis* and *Elevatio Crucis* (No. 7) from a Vadstena Processional (Uppsala Universitets Biblioteket, MS. C. 506, fol. b ii [10ᵛ]).

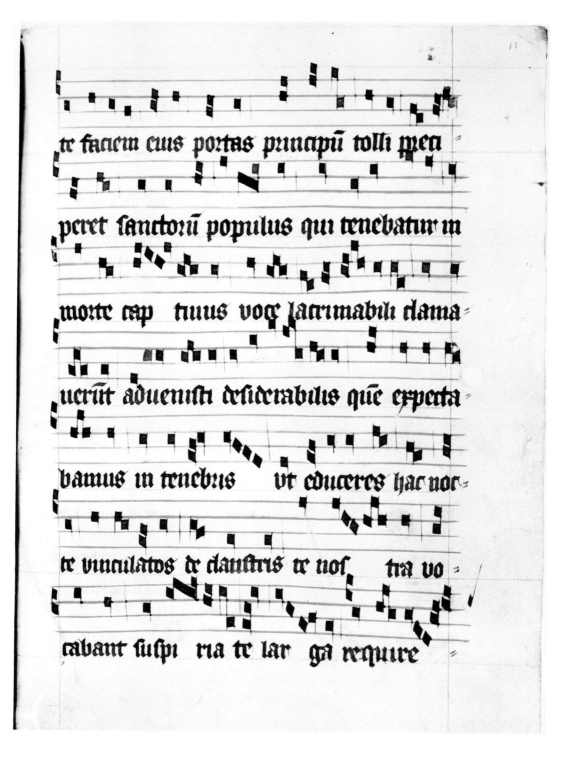

16. Continuation of *Depositio Crucis* and *Elevatio Crucis* (No. 7) from a Vadstena Processional (Uppsala Universitets Biblioteket, MS. C. 506, fol. b iii [11ʳ]).

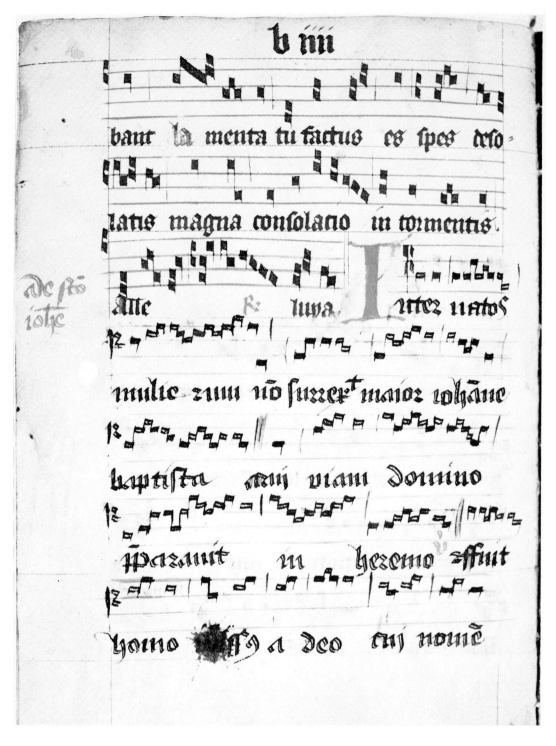

17. Conclusion of *Elevatio Crucis* (No. 7) from a Vadstena Processional (Uppsala Universitets Biblioteket, MS. C. 506, fol. b iv [11ᵛ]).

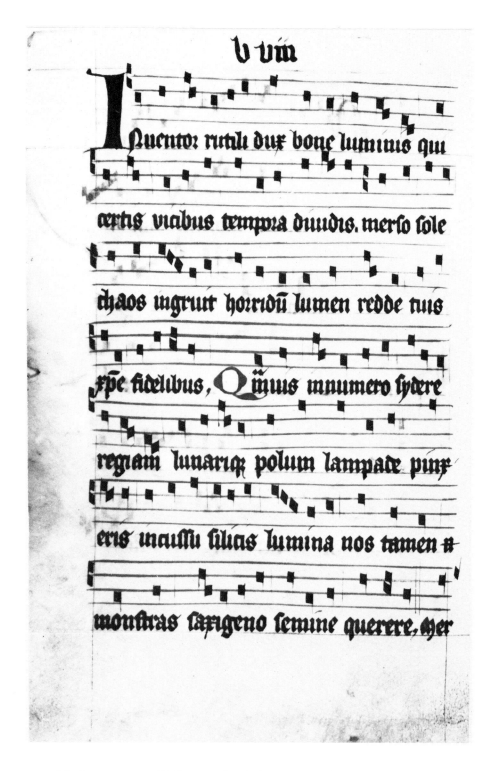

18. *Inuentor rutili* (incomplete) from Uppsala Universitets Biblioteket, MS. C. 506, fol. b viii (15ᵛ).